ALASTAIR NOBLE

FOREIGN & COMMONWEALTH OFFICE

DOCUMENTS ON BRITISH POLICY OVERSEAS

EDITED BY

KEITH HAMILTON

AND

PATRICK SALMON

ASSISTED BY

CHRISTOPHER BAXTER

AND

ALASTAIR NOBLE

SERIES III

Volume IV

Routledge
Taylor & Francis Group

LONDON AND NEW YORK

First published 2006
by Routledge
2 Park Square, Milton Park, Abingdon, Oxon OX14 4RN

Simultaneously published in the USA and Canada
by Routledge
270 Madison Ave, New York, NY 10016

Routledge is an imprint of the Taylor & Francis Group, an informa business

© 2006 Crown Copyright

Printed and bound in Great Britain by Biddles Ltd, King's Lynn

*Published on behalf of the Whitehall History Publishing Consortium.
Applications to reproduce Crown copyright protected material in this
publication should be submitted in writing to: HMSO, Copyright Unit,
St Clements House, 2-16 Colegate, Norwich NR3 1BQ.
Fax: 01603 723000. E-mail: copyright@hmso.gov.uk*

Publisher's note
This book has been produced from camera-ready copy supplied by the author.

British Library Cataloguing in Publication Data
A catalogue record for this book is available from the British Library

Library of Congress Cataloging in Publication Data
A catalog record for this book has been requested

ISBN10: 0–415–39150–4 (pack)
ISBN10: 0–415–39149–0 (hbk)

ISBN13: 978–0–415–39150–4 (pack)
ISBN13: 978–0–415–39149–8 (hbk)

DOCUMENTS ON BRITISH POLICY OVERSEAS

Series III, Volume IV

The Year of Europe: America, Europe and the Energy Crisis, 1972–1974

WHITEHALL HISTORIES: FOREIGN AND COMMONWEALTH OFFICE PUBLICATIONS
Series Editors: Keith Hamilton and Patrick Salmon
ISSN: 1471-2083

FCO historians are responsible for editing *Documents on British Policy Overseas* (DBPO) and for overseeing the publication of FCO Internal Histories.

DBPO comprises three series of diplomatic documents, focusing on major themes in foreign policy since 1945, and drawn principally from the records of the Foreign and Commonwealth Office. The latest volumes, published in Series III, contain archival material which would otherwise be unavailable to the public.

FCO Internal Histories are occasional studies by former serving officials, commissioned to provide background information for members of the FCO, to point out possible lessons for the future and to evaluate how well objectives were met in a particular episode or crisis. They are not written for publication, but some Internal Histories, which offer fresh insights into British diplomacy, are now being declassified for publication by Whitehall History Publishing in association with Routledge.

Latest published volumes:

Britain and China, 1945-1950
Documents on British Policy Overseas, Series I, Volume VIII
S.R. Ashton, G. Bennett and K.A. Hamilton (eds)

Britain and the Soviet Union, 1968-1972
Documents on British Policy Overseas, Series III, Volume I
G. Bennett and K.A. Hamilton (eds)

The Conference on Security and Cooperation in Europe, 1972-1975
Documents on British Policy Overseas, Series III, Volume II
G. Bennett and K.A. Hamilton (eds)

Détente in Europe, 1972-1976
Documents on British Policy Overseas, Series III, Volume III
G. Bennett and K.A. Hamilton (eds)

Forthcoming volume:

The Southern Flank in Crisis, 1973-1976
Documents on British Policy Overseas, Series III, Volume V
K.A. Hamilton and P. Salmon (eds)

CD-ROMs

The CD-ROMs should auto-start. If they do not, follow the instructions below:

- Open 'My Computer'
- Read the drive for your CD-ROM player
- Locate file "Start.pdf" and double-click

System Requirements:

- Use of a PC
- Adobe Reader 6.0 - can be downloaded free of charge from the Adobe website *www.adobe.co.uk* or via the Help menu in your current Adobe Reader.

Note: The Autoplay software installed on the CD-ROMs is not compatible with MAC computers.

PREFACE

Three years ago the Editors of *Documents on British Policy Overseas* (DBPO) decided to explore the possibility of compiling a volume of documents in electronic format, rather than in convential book form. It was felt that this would provide the public with easier access to Britain's diplomatic record and that it would appeal to an academic community increasingly accustomed to working with computerised resources. Scholars and others interested in the making and conduct of British foreign policy could thereby be provided with a much larger number of documents than would otherwise be available in hard copy, and the documents would be fully searchable and could be reproduced in facsimile for research and teaching purposes. It was also assumed that by dispensing with some of the more detailed explanatory material, which must necessarily accompany a smaller selection of documents, Foreign and Commonwealth Office (FCO) Historians would be able to hasten volume production. Readers would not be provided with the contextual cross-referencing, which has been a key feature of hard-copy volumes, but they would have the satisfaction of being able to view many more documents as they appear in sequence on file.

The two accompanying CD-ROMs, containing some 568 scanned documents, constitute the electronic component of this series III volume. They focus on transatlantic relations during Britain's first year as a member of the European Community, and cover British reactions to the launch in 1973 of the Nixon Administration's 'Year of Europe' initiative, and the impact on the Atlantic Alliance of the fourth Arab-Israeli War and the Energy Crisis. To assist readers, brief summaries of the documents are here reproduced in printed text, along with an historical introduction to the volume, and lists of abbreviations and persons cited in the documents.

Acknowledgements

In accordance with the Parliamentary announcement cited in the Preface to Series I, Volume I of DBPO, the Editors have had the customary freedom in the selection and arrangement of documents including full access to all classes of FCO documentation. There have, in the case of the present volume, been no exceptional cases, such as were provided for in the Parliamentary announcement, where it has been necessary on security grounds to restrict the availability of particular documents, editorially selected in accordance with regular practice.

The main source of documentation in this volume has been the archives of the FCO, including papers originating with other Whitehall Departments. Most of the documents were consulted prior to their transfer to The National Archives (TNA). As indicated in the document summaries below, twelve documents were selected from FCO files which were subsequently destroyed because they did not meet the criteria of TNA's acquisition policy. These have been scanned and reproduced on CD-ROM from photocopies made at the pre-selection stage. The papers of Sir Alec Douglas-Home and Sir Thomas Brimelow, which proved a valuable supplementary source, await transfer. Other documents included on the CD-ROM, and already in the public domain, were selected from Cabinet Office records. In providing access to these records and for help in locating specific files, we are grateful to Mrs Heather Yasamee, Assistant Director and Head of the FCO's Information Management Group, and her staff, particularly Miss Margaret Ryan and Mrs Caroline Puddephatt, presently of, and Mrs Ann Birch, formerly of, Records Retrieval, and those in Library Information Services who have dealt with our many queries. We should also like to thank Ms Gill Bennett, who, prior to her retirement as the FCO's Chief Historian, was responsible for supervising the project; Dr Martin Longden, formerly of FCO Historians, who contributed much to its inception; Dr Christopher Baxter for his continuing administrative support; Ms Hala Bouguerne, our ever-resilient Publications Manager, Mr Eamonn Clifford, her immediate predecessor, and their assistants Mr Kewal Rai and Mr Craig Buchan, for their technical expertise; and Ms Sally Falk of the Histories, Openness and Records Section of the Cabinet Office, and Professor Geoffrey Berridge of the University of Leicester, both of whom aided and facilitated our researches. We are, however, especially indebted to Dr Alastair Noble, whose industry, intellectual curiosity and perseverence have proved so important to the completion of this work.

KEITH HAMILTON
PATRICK SALMON

June 2005

CONTENTS

ABBREVIATIONS

ABM — Anti-Ballistic Missile
AP/AFP — Associated Foreign Press
APS — Assistant Private Secretary
ARAMCO — Arabian American Oil Company
ASU — Arab Socialist Union
AUS — Assistant Under-Secretary of State
BP — British Petroleum
BRITAIRAT — British Air Attaché
BRITDEFAT — British Defence Attaché
C20 — Committee of the IMF's Board of Governors on Reform of the International Monetary System
CAP — Common Agricultural Policy
CBFNE — Commander British Forces Near East
CIEP — Council on International Economic Policy
CMEA/COMECON COCOM — Council for Mutual Economic Assistance Coordinating Committee for Multilateral Export Controls
COD — Communications Operations Department, FCO
CONS D — Consular Department, FCO
CONS E UNIT — Consular Emergency Unit, FCO
COREPER — *Comité des Representants Permanents*/Committee of Permanent Representatives
CPRS — Central Policy Review Staff, Cabinet Office
CPSU — Communist Party of the Soviet Union
CPX — Command Post Exercise
CSCE — Conference on Security and Cooperation in Europe
CSD — Civil Service Department
despt — despatch
DISCS — Domestic International Sales Corporations
DOP — Defence and Oversea Policy Committee of the Cabinet
DPC — Defence Planning Committee, NATO
DTI — Department of Trade and Industry
DUS — Deputy Under-Secretary of State
EAG — Energy Action Group
EC — European Community/Communities
EDF — European Development Fund
EDIP — European Defence Improvement Programme
EEC — European Economic Community
EESD — Eastern European and Soviet Department, FCO
EFTA — European Free Trade Area
EID (E)/(I) — European Integration Department (Exernal)/(Internal)

EMU	European Monetary Union	IRD	Information Research Department, FCO
EN D	Energy Department, FCO	ISA	International Security Affairs, US Department of Defense
EPC	European Political Cooperation	ISED	Industry, Science and Energy Department, FCO
EUM	Cabinet Ministerial Committee on Europe		
EURONAD	European National Armament Directors, NATO	JIC	Joint Intelligence Committee
		JISNE	Joint Intelligence Staff Near East
FBS	Forward Based [Nuclear Delivery] Systems	LDC	Least/Less Developed Country/Countries
FCO	Foreign and Commonwealth Office	MAFF	Ministry of Agriculture, Fisheries and Food
FED	Far Eastern Department, FCO	MBFR	Mutual and Balanced Force Reductions
FRD	Financial Relations Department, FCO	MED	Middle East Department, FCO
FRG	Federal Republic of Germany	memo	memorandum
		MFA	Ministry of Foreign Affairs
FSO	Foreign Service Officer		
GATT	General Agreement on Tariffs and Trade	MFN	Most Favoured Nation
		MIFT	My immediately following telegram
GCHQ	Government Communications Headquarters		
		MIPT	My immediately preceding telegram
GIPD	Guidance and Information Policy Department, FCO	MIRV	Multiple Independently-Targetable Re-entry Vehicle
GNP	Gross National Product	MITI	Ministry of International Trade and Industry, Japan
GSP	Gross State Product		
HKIOD	Hong Kong and Indian Ocean Department, FCO	MoD/ MODUK	Ministry of Defence
HLG	High Level Group, OECD	MRCA	Multi-Role Combat Aircraft
HMG	Her Majesty's Government	MTD	Maritime and Transport Department, FCO
IAF	Israeli Air Force		
IDF	Israeli Defence Forces	mtg	meeting
IFT	Immediately following telegram	NAC	North Atlantic Council
		NAD/ N AM D	North America Department, FCO
IMF	International Monetary Fund		FCO

NATO	North Atlantic Treaty Organisation		FCO
NENAD	Near East and North Africa Department, FCO	RID	Republic of Ireland Department, FCO
NIO	Northern Ireland Office	SACEUR	Supreme Allied Commander, Europe
NPG	Nuclear Planning Group, NATO	SACLANT	Supreme Allied Commander, Atlantic
NSC	National Security Council	SAD	South Asian Department, FCO
NTB	Non-tariff Barriers	SALT	Strategic Arms Limitation Talks
OAPEC	Organisation of Arab Petroleum Exporting Countries	SDR	Special Drawing Rights
		SED	Southern European Department, FCO
OECD	Organisation for Economic Cooperation and Development	SPC	Senior Political Committee, NATO
		STD	Science and Technology Department, FCO
OPEC	Organisation of Petroleum Exporting Countries	SWPD	South West Pacific Department, FCO
OPIC	Organisation of Petroleum Importing Countries	tel	telegram
		TRED	Trade Relations and Exports Department, FCO
Pdq	Pretty damn quick[ly]		
PDRY	People's Democratic Republic of the Yemen	TUR	Telegram under reference
POD	Personnel Operations Department, FCO	UKDEL	United Kingdom Delegation
PPD	Personnel Policy Department, FCO	UKMIS	United Kingdom Mission
PPS	Principal Private Secretary	UKREP	United Kingdom Representative
PRISEC	Private Secretary to the Secretary of State, FCO	UN	United Nations
		UND	UN Department, FCO
		UNEF	UN Emergency Force in the Middle East
PQ	Parliamentary Question		
PS	Private Secretary	UNGA	UN General Assembly
PUS	Permanent Under-Secretary of State	UNMO	UN Military Observers
		UNSC	UN Security Council
PUSD	Permanent Under-Secretary's Department, FCO	VSOP	Working Party on Vast Oil Surpluses
		WED	Western European Department, FCO
RDF	Regional Development Fund	WOD	Western Organisations Department, FCO
RES D	Research Department,		

INTRODUCTION

The Nixon Administration designated 1973 the 'Year of Europe' (No. 51). But in the words of Lord Cromer, Britain's Ambassador in Washington, the year 'failed to live up to its advanced billing' (No. 432). What began as an American initiative aimed at redefining relations between the United States and Western Europe and reasserting the values and interests they shared in common, ended in a fractious debate over the drafting of two seemingly innocuous declarations. A projected presidential visit to Europe failed to materialise, and Henry Kissinger, President Nixon's National Security Adviser, took umbrage at the less than enthusiastic reception given by the Europeans to his call for a new 'Atlantic Charter'. Meanwhile, the mixed responses of America's allies to the outbreak of war in the Middle East and divergent approaches to the ensuing energy crisis threatened the unity of NATO and exposed serious deficiencies in the policy-making processes of the newly-enlarged European Community (EC). America's selective bilateralism on the world stage was matched by France's predictable exceptionalism in Europe. The United Kingdom, which, along with Denmark and the Republic of Ireland, became a fully-fledged member of the EC on 1 January 1973, found itself in the invidious position of trying to maintain its 'special' or 'natural' relationship with the United States while at the same time seeking to demonstrate to its continental neighbours its commitment to the construction of a European union from whose counsels the Americans would be excluded. This volume documents the reactions of British statesmen and diplomats to these developments, and their contribution to promoting the notion of a European identity founded on cooperation, rather than competition, with the United States. It focuses on the strains and stresses affecting inter-allied relations as a result of institutional change, overseas conflict, and economic turbulence in the period between the Paris summit of EC Heads of State and Government of 19-20 October 1972 and the Washington Energy Conference of 11-12 February 1974.

Mid-Atlantic Diplomacy
EC enlargement inevitably impacted upon transatlantic relations. At the Paris summit the six present and three prospective member-states, while affirming 'their intention to transform before the end of the ... decade the whole complex of their relations into a European Union' with a distinct personality, agreed that they would remain faithful to Europe's traditional friendships and their existing alliances.[1] Ten days later, in a personal letter

---

[1] Cmnd 5109, *The European Communities. Text of the Communiqué issued by the Heads of State or of Government of the Countries of the enlarged Community at their Meeting in Paris on the 19th and 20th of October 1972* (London: HMSO, 1973), p. 4.

to President Nixon of 30 October 1972 Edward Heath, the British Prime Minister, wrote that he was determined to ensure that the long-term relationship between the Community and the United States was 'constructed so as to correspond with our real interest in maintaining the closest possible ties' (No. 1). Adjustments would however have to be made in the commercial sphere and, following Washington's suspension of dollar convertibility in August 1971, these must be effected against a background of international financial uncertainty. The summit communiqué foresaw the establishment of an economic and monetary union in Europe by December 1980[2] and, although mention was made of the need to maintain a constructive dialogue with the United States, Japan and Canada on world trade problems, it was predictable that in the forthcoming round of talks on the General Agreement on Tariffs and Trade (GATT) the Americans would be looking for compensation for losses they believed themselves likely to incur as a result of the extension of the EC's tariff régime to Britain, Denmark and Ireland. As Cromer pointed out in a despatch of 15 November, the recently re-elected Nixon Administration had 'the political objective of a strong Western Alliance and a balanced relationship between the US and the enlarged European Community', but 'the economic objective of reversing a vast trade deficit'. Americans tended to regard the EC and its widening network of associated states as a closed economic bloc; they viewed its Common Agricultural Policy (CAP) as unfair to US agriculture; and they considered its preferential trading arrangements as a derogation from GATT (No. 2).

The British, in Cromer's opinion, faced peculiarly difficult tactical problems in seeking to ensure that relations between the enlarged Community and the United States started off on the basis of friendship rather than antagonism. 'At this end', he noted, 'no one would under-estimate the great obstacles presented by the existence of protectionist attitudes and by pressures for reduced expenditure on defence, by the temptations to the US to deal bilaterally with the Soviet Union and to the Western Europeans to concentrate on building their union' (*ibid.*). Lord Carrington, the Defence Secretary, expressed similar fears. From a European standpoint, the Americans appeared to view the international scene increasingly in terms of their super-power relationship with the Soviet Union, and their military withdrawal from Vietnam and evident desire to achieve an early settlement there were hardly calculated to inspire confidence amongst their allies (No. 3). Yet of more immediate concern to British diplomats in the autumn of 1972 was the practical question of how best to ensure that on specifically Community matters, such as trade and finance, member-states and the EC Commission spoke with one voice in their dealings with the United States. With a prime ministerial visit to Washington scheduled for early in 1973, Robert Armstrong, Heath's Principal Private Secretary, wondered whether the time might have come

[2] Cmnd 5109, pp. 4-6.

for setting up 'continuing arrangements' whereby problems could be 'discussed' between the EC and the US. True, the French had objected to the idea on the grounds that 'it would too greatly institutionalise the relationship', but, as Armstrong observed, the opposite danger· was that in the absence of such arrangements, the Americans would find it 'too easy to "divide and rule" the Community' (No. 4).

Cromer found the Americans 'understandably schizophrenic on whether they want[ed] to see Europe speaking with one voice or to conduct bilateral discussions with capitals' (No. 2). Moreover, as he explained in a letter of 19 January 1973 to Sir Denis Greenhill, the Permanent Under-Secretary (PUS) at the Foreign and Commonwealth Office (FCO), they would be inclined to treat relations with Europe as 'one ball of wax', emphasising the linkage between monetary, trade and defence issues and, in the context of the Atlantic Alliance, looking for greater burden-sharing (No. 14). This approach presented serious difficulties for the Europeans. The nine EC member-states were at different stages as regards achieving common positions in the three fields concerned, and organisationally different people and institutions dealt with them, nationally, within Europe, bilaterally with the United States and multilaterally. The Nine were, for instance, committed to the reform of the international monetary system, yet they were far from agreed on such matters as the future role of gold; and the fact that EC membership was not synonymous with European membership of NATO was bound to complicate negotiations in the defence sphere. At a meeting of EC Political Directors on 16 January to discuss Nixon's 'forthcoming visit to Europe' for what a White House spokesman had already referred to as the 'Year of Europe',[3] there was general agreement that negotiations in the three spheres should be kept separate and in their several institutions (No. 12). There should in other words be no globalisation of issues.

Relations between the United States and the Community figured large in wide-ranging discussions which Heath had with Nixon in Washington and at Camp David during 1-2 February (Nos. 20-22). The visit followed the conclusion in Paris on 27 January of an agreement aimed at bringing an end to the ten-year old war in Vietnam, and coincided with an upheaval

---

[3] Kissinger first gave rise to the expectation of a presidential visit to Europe during a press conference in London on 16 September 1972. Then, following talks with Heath, Kissinger said that Nixon, if re-elected, would undertake some striking new initiative towards Europe, probably in the form of another tour of European capitals. He added that he had been asked by Nixon to point out to European leaders that 'he hoped to resume most intense consultations with our European friends on how to put relationships between Europe and the United States on a new even more dynamic and constructive basis, consistent with the change in the international situation'. Draft Planning Staff paper, 'Transatlantic Relations: Record of Events to July 1973', attached to a minute of 21 September 1973 from James Cable (Head of Planning Staff) to Antony Acland (Principal Private Secretary to the Secretary of State) (RS 2/3, annex). Cable's minute and an accompanying analysis of the impact of 'Year of Europe' initiative are reproduced at No. 231.

on the world currency markets and a fresh fall in the value of the US dollar. It was therefore hardly surprising that while the first session of talks was devoted mainly to the problems of South-East Asia,[4] the second was concerned with international commercial and financial matters. While Nixon was personally grateful to the British Government for its refusal to join other European Governments in condemning America's resumed bombing of North Vietnam in the previous December, George Shultz, his Treasury Secretary, impressed on Heath the importance the Administration attached to Britain giving a new direction to the European approach to GATT (No. 20). The message was clear: a new US trade bill was in preparation and if the Europeans wished to avoid restrictive legislation they must be seen to be adopting a less rigid stance. Nixon likewise reminded Heath of the Congressional pressure he was facing to reduce US force numbers in Europe (No. 22). As Hugh Overton, Head of the FCO's North American Department (NAD), subsequently explained, the White House tended 'to see the European nations as weak, selfish, indecisive and suspicious of US motives, and hence a pretty unrewarding lot to try to manage'. But 'even allowing for hyperbole and perhaps some desire to divide and rule', the British were still seen as 'America's staunchest and most dependable ally' (No. 25). It was, Cromer observed, a great relief to Nixon that Britain was joining the EC under a Prime Minister who held the views Heath did. 'Indeed', he added with some prescience, 'such is the trust of President Nixon that therein lie the seeds of disillusion in the future, on occasions when Community policy, which will of course embrace British policy, is at variance with American thinking' (No. 29).

The notion of a 'Year of Europe' doubtless owed much to Kissinger's belief that US foreign policy had for so long been focused upon Vietnam and improving relations with the Soviet Union and Communist China, that America's NATO allies must be feeling neglected. European governments were, as Heath suggested to Nixon and Kissinger at Camp David on 2 February, concerned at not being kept fully informed of Washington's dealings with Moscow. Kissinger's secret diplomacy was not best suited to the maintenance of allied solidarity. And Nixon's observation to Heath that Britain and the US must 'do some really hard thinking together—without necessarily telling the rest of the Alliance at any particular stage but keeping privately in step and moving publicly, if not together, at least in parallel', hardly suggested any change of practice. The British were, however, already party to one of the more occult of Kissinger's endeavours—his negotiation with the Russians of the Agreement, signed in Washington on 22 June 1973, on the Prevention of Nuclear War. News that the Soviet Union had proposed such an understanding was first revealed to Sir Burke Trend, the Cabinet Secretary, when at Kissinger's request he

---

[4] Record of a Discussion at the White House, Washington, on 1 February 1973, AMU 3/548/8.

4

visited Washington on 28 July 1972,[5] for an exchange of 'general views on the world situation'.[6] The British had serious misgivings about the project which, by removing the main nuclear threat to the Soviet Union, might clear the decks for Soviet action by conventional forces against China, severely weaken NATO, and create a political climate in which it would be difficult for Britain to develop further its own deterrent. On 10 August Sir Thomas Brimelow, Deputy Under-Secretary of State (DUS) in the FCO, communicated these to Kissinger. Anxious, however, not to rebuff the Soviet initiative, and wishing to respond with a counter-proposal consistent with Western security requirements, Kissinger invited Brimelow to assist in drafting a revised text. Moreover, although the resulting text was rejected by the Russians as insufficient, Nixon argued strongly in favour of holding open the prospect of such a deal in order 'to keep the Soviet Union in play and at the same time to fend off, month by month, Congressional pressure for United States troop reductions in Europe'.[7]

No one outside the White House was initially informed of the proposed accord, and British involvement in its drafting, code-named 'Operation Hullabaloo', bordered on the bizarre. Brimelow was in effect to become Kissinger's desk-officer for the Soviet Union, amending and putting into treaty form a bilateral US/Soviet arrangement for which he had little personal sympathy (Nos. 15, 17 and 32). Cromer summarised the situation pithily when, following a visit from Brimelow for talks with Kissinger on 5 March, he noted how he was 'struck by the astonishing anomaly of the most powerful nation in the world invoking the aid of a foreign government to do its drafting for it, while totally excluding its own Ministry for Foreign Affairs' (No. 44). Of course this had the advantage of allowing Brimelow and his colleagues the opportunity to influence the outcome of the US/Soviet dialogue, and their drafting helped ensure that the agreement left America's commitment to its NATO allies largely unimpaired. Emphasis in the agreement was thus shifted away from the non-use of nuclear weapons and towards the creation of 'conditions in which the recourse to nuclear weapons [would] not be justified' (Nos. 59-61, 95 and 131). Yet, as Cromer reminded Brimelow, there were dangers in these proceedings, particularly given 'the highly devious nature of

---

[5] During discussions with Nixon in Bermuda on 20-21 December 1971, Heath agreed with the President that contact between the United States and its Western European allies on current issues and policy was inadequate and that the habit of consultation should be developed. Heath also stated that Britain 'did not intend to pursue a pro-European policy—she intended to pursue the policy which best served British interests and these included maintaining the closest links between the two sides of the Atlantic'. One consequence of this assurance was that US/European relations were added to the agenda of intermittent bilateral talks already proceeding between Trend and Kissinger, knowledge of which was restricted to a very small circle in London. See note 3 above.

[6] Record of discussions with Dr Kissinger in Washington on 28 July 1972, AMU 3/548/12.

[7] Records of conversations with Dr Kissinger in Washington on 10 August, and in London on 14 September, 1972, Brimelow Papers.

Kissinger's intellectual make-up'. Although Kissinger indicated that Bonn and Paris had been told of the Soviet approach, neither was apparently aware of the American response, and Britain would be vulnerable to criticism from its European partners if they were ever to learn of Brimelow's role in the affair (No. 44).

The British risked similar embarrassment in replying to a further proposal which Kissinger put to Brimelow on 5 March. Kissinger then said, with reference to the Atlantic Alliance, that the US Government would like to elaborate common views on political content, military doctrine and the economic aspects of the relationship. And to this end, he invited Britain to work with the United States in closest consultation in devising a 'conceptual framework' to be borne in mind in future dealings with the Soviet Union (*ibid.*). Heath agreed that British officials 'should certainly go along with the enterprise in principle, albeit keeping a weather eye on the reactions of [their] European allies'. They would, as Trend noted, have to 'be on [their] guard against any suggestion that [they were] "ganging up" with the Americans against Europe'.[8] Ministers and senior officials also retained doubts about Kissinger's all-embracing 'one ball of wax' concept when applied to the political, defence and economic aspects of transatlantic relations, and amendments made to Brimelow's first draft of a 'framework paper' addressed their concerns (No. 62). The resulting paper, 'The Next Ten Years in East-West and Trans-Atlantic Relations', was, as the accompanying speaking notes made clear, 'conceived as a "mid-Atlantic" statement of assumptions and of questions arising from them', whose emphasis on the political and strategic aspects of East-West relations did not fully reflect European preoccupations and priorities. It thus assumed that the US interest in maintaining Western unity against the Soviet Union would have to be balanced against an American interest in reducing defence costs, and that, while the economic integration and political solidarity of the EC was likely to grow faster than expected, NATO's European members would not be ready to take on as much of the common defence burden as the US would wish (No. 65).

The paper, which was despatched to Washington on 12 April for Cromer's communication to Kissinger, went on to pose a series of questions covering the inter-relationship between defence, monetary and trade problems. Yet, as was only too apparent to its authors, there simply was no means for handling these in a single forum. There also remained the possibility that the US Administration might seek to use this linkage 'only to strengthen American bargaining positions on each of the three subjects'. This they felt would be a pity, particularly since the dynamic integration of Western Europe would help convince the Russians that they could not hope to divide the Europeans from one another, and they should also be denied the hope of dividing the Europeans from the United States. The speaking notes made a simple, if somewhat optimistic point: 'All the

---

[8] Minute from Trend to Heath of 16 March 1973, CAB 164/1232.

West European governments, France included, now want a calm and cooperative relationship between the US and Europe. This is equally important to the United States' (*ibid.*). Despite, however, the time and effort which went into preparing the British conceptual framework paper, Kissinger appeared not to have studied it in any detail when on 19 April he met with Cromer, Trend, Brimelow and other British officials in Washington for four hours of discussion. Although he admitted that he agreed with a great deal of it, his comments tended towards the negative: he objected to its 'tone of mild fatalism' and to its 'lack of sense of dynamism'. Yet he had little that was positive or new to suggest. He spoke again of his desire to give 'symbolic impetus' to the transatlantic relationship, and of the need to find some way of making it 'an "emotional necessity" to United States public opinion'. Could they not, he asked, find some way of rationalising the issue by subjecting it to systematic study by a series of working parties, which would examine its various implications under the direction of some kind of steering committee? In addition, Kissinger pressed for a 'radical reappraisal of NATO strategy—with all its political and financial implications' (Nos. 69 and 75).

Much of the discussion in Washington was concerned with what were essentially strategic matters, and Kissinger referred only briefly to the economic differences between America and Europe. He insisted, however, that these must be form part of a global approach (*ibid.*). Unfortunately, they seemed unlikely to lend themselves to early resolution. Already in a memorandum of 5 March Sir Geoffrey Howe, the Minister for Trade and Consumer Affairs, warned his colleagues that unless the EC were able to offer the Americans compensation for the losses they believed themselves to be incurring as a result of Community enlargement, they faced the real possibility of a trade war with all its political repercussions. Britain must therefore persuade other member-states to make concessions, particularly on agriculture (No. 41). Heath hardly needed reminding about American sensitivities regarding European economic cooperation. Despite its devaluation by 10% in February, the US dollar once more came under pressure in early March. European money markets closed, and during talks between Heath and his West German opposite number, Willy Brandt, in Bonn on 1-2 March both the Prime Minister and the Federal Chancellor explored the possibility of a joint float of EC currencies (No. 37). In a subsequent personal message to Nixon, Brandt wrote that he and Heath had agreed that they must make every conceivable effort to find a way out of the currency crisis which 'strengthen[ed] European integration'. The choice of words was infelicitous and prompted a tetchy personal protest from Nixon to Heath that the United States could not accept the proposition that European integration was the 'sole criterion' to be considered in putting forward a solution (No. 38). Heath accepted the point, but replied that many in Europe believed the ability of EC member-states to work out and agree a joint solution was a 'crucial test' of the Community's purpose (No. 39).

Much, however, to Heath's disappointment, Britain was unable to participate in the joint European float established as a result of a meeting of EC Finance Ministers on 11 March. Its partners considered proposals involving unlimited and unconditional credit on a Community basis too far-reaching, and without such a commitment neither the Treasury nor the Bank of England reckoned that the pound sterling, which had been floated in June 1972, could risk returning to a fixed parity régime (Nos. 48-50). Britain's economic weakness, its balance of payments problems and relatively high rate of inflation, seemed likely to diminish its political influence in the Community, and this in turn threatened to impair commercial relations with the United States. On 19 March the French President, Georges Pompidou, expressed the opinion that unless Britain entered the EC's monetary 'snake' there could be no further progress towards economic and monetary union and no agreement on multilateral trade negotiations (Nos. 53 and 54). Meanwhile, the US Administration proceeded with its Trade Reform Bill, legislation which was intended to provide Nixon with wide discretionary powers for just such negotiations (No. 56). As Cromer explained, after the Bill's publication, it was not in essence a protectionist measure, 'although it [had] many "clubs in the closet"'. Nixon, he observed, was only interested in trade reform in so far as a strong US economy provided an essential basis to his and Kissinger's grand political designs (No. 68). One of these, their plan to reaffirm Atlantic solidarity with 'something more than the "traditional liturgies"', was to be launched by Kissinger on 23 April with a speech, the general purport of which was revealed to Trend and his colleagues on 19 April, to the annual luncheon of Associated Press. It was, Kissinger told Trend, 'prompted by the President's conviction that, unless the essential basis of Atlantic unity could be reconstituted, everything would go wrong'. He hoped therefore for a positive British response immediately after its delivery (Nos. 69, 70 and 75).

A New Atlantic Charter

In his speech of 23 April Kissinger sought to define and give philosophical content to what he understood by the 'Year of Europe' (No. 72). He spoke of a world in transition, of the movement of Europe towards economic unification, of the shift in the East-West relationship from American preponderance to near equality, of the relaxation of tensions, of the emergence of Japan as a major power centre, and of whether an Atlantic unity 'forged by a common perception of danger [could] draw new purpose from shared positive aspirations'. And with this in view, he proposed that by the time the President travelled to Europe towards the end of the year, the United States and its Atlantic partners should have worked out a 'new Atlantic Charter setting the goals for the future'—a relationship, moreover, in whose progress he hoped Japan could share. He spoke also of the linkage between various policy issues, of the need for mutual concessions in the economic sphere, of the Administration's desire for a 'new consensus on security', and of maintaining the 'momentum of détente ... by common objectives rather than by, drift, escapism or complacency'. 'The U.S.', Kissinger observed, 'has global interests and responsibilities. Our European allies have regional interests. These are not necessarily in conflict, but in the new era neither are they automatically identical.' If the Atlantic nations wanted to foster unity, they must, he insisted, 'find a solution for the management of their diversity', and identify 'interests and positive values beyond security in order to engage once again the commitment of peoples and parliaments' (No. 70).

The speech was evidently in part intended to undercut the arguments of those pressing for America's adoption of more protectionist measures and for cuts in US forces in Europe. Yet, as Cromer emphasised, the Administration was also looking for a favourable reaction from Europe to the spirit of the speech, and if this were forthcoming it 'could have a similar influence in terms of its effect on the detailed development of US policy to the constructive British response to Marshall's historic offer in 1948'. If on the other hand the European reaction were 'crabbed', there was a danger of the initiative falling flat (No. 71). Sir Alec Douglas-Home, the Foreign and Commonwealth Secretary, responded quickly, authorising the FCO's News Department to release a statement welcoming Kissinger's acknowledgement of the concept of a unified Europe working cooperatively with the United States (No. 77). But there was also some uncertainty in London over what exactly Kissinger had in mind when he spoke of a new Atlantic Charter, and very little enthusiasm for the implied assumption that a package solution could be found to outstanding differences over defence, trade and monetary matters. In a speech at Dunblane on 27 April Douglas-Home, while endorsing Kissinger's language as 'realistic and timely', said that he would have preferred the EC to have had more time in which to 'find its way to common positions with greater deliberation' (No. 79). Moreover, although most of Britain's EC partners agreed that a common European approach should be adopted to relations with America, the French clearly had the gravest reservations about what Kissinger had had to say (No. 78). Sir Edward Tomkins, the British Ambassador at Paris, reported that there was a feeling in the Quai d'Orsay that the Kissinger proposal was 'mainly a tactical ploy, designed to put American demands on the table in advance of the forthcoming negotiations and to put Europe on the defensive'. French officials regarded Kissinger's reference to the United States having a 'world role' compared with the 'regional responsibilities of Europe' as patronising, and his presentation likely to make the task of reaching an agreement on political and economic questions more difficult (No. 75).

In a minute to Heath of 2 May Trend pointed out that the French were unlikely to be sympathetic towards the idea of a close link between the United States and Europe. '[W]e', he noted, 'must be wary of any United States attempt to drive a political wedge between ourselves and our European allies or to use us as a stalking horse for Washington's purposes in Europe'. Indeed, while he thought that Britain must respond to the speech in as 'positive and constructive a manner as possible', he considered it preferable that the United States 'having launched this project, should also be responsible for following it up and making the running for at least the next round or two' (No. 81). British diplomats were in any case doubtful as to whether the French would be prepared to discuss Kissinger's initiative with their European partners until after a meeting between Pompidou and Nixon scheduled for the end of May (No. 86). Yet, as Cromer warned Brimelow in a letter of 8 May, Nixon would be 'disillusioned' if Europe failed at least to examine the proposal in the same constructive spirit as it had been made. He suggested that Europeans should aim at producing a broad Declaration of Principles designed to show the contrast between life in the West and that in communist societies, and that this might be followed by a 'series of actions to put flesh on its bones'. The initial work in Europe should, he thought, be done by the Nine, and this, he hoped, would 'lead to an increase in consultation and cooperation in all matters of foreign policy without which, however close economic and monetary cooperation may become, union [would] never be achieved' (No. 87).

Overton also favoured a positive, though gradualist, European response. Nixon's weakened domestic position, the result of revelations regarding the Watergate affair, had, Overton argued, left him in need of a foreign policy success, and had thereby strengthened Europe's bargaining position. The Nine should, he minuted, 'adopt a sympathetic and constructive stance but play things cool and long, decline to be hustled, and progressively force the Americans to redefine their objectives in face of the difficulties' (No. 88). That said, Overton feared that references in Kissinger's speech to the link between defence, trade and monetary issues threatened to 'embitter US/Europe relations at a critical and formative stage in the dialogue' (No. 97). The French were certainly insistent that there could be no such linkage. During a meeting with Kissinger on 17 May Michel Jobert, the French Foreign Minister, maintained that 'when it came to negotiations about specific problems these should be conducted separately in the various forums which were appropriate' (No. 96). Heath likewise found Pompidou, with whom he had talks on 21-22 May, 'preoccupied by the institutional aspect' of handling the American initiative. On relations between the Nine and the United States, Pompidou contended that an EC/US declaration could only be made within the scope of the Community's competences, and that its scope would therefore be limited and could not have the general content of bilateral state-to-state relationships. He also rejected the idea of a meeting between Nixon and the Council of Ministers as a whole during the President's projected visit to Europe in the autumn. The French Government, he said, had no intention of involving itself in 'a kind of "court circle"', and that at a Community level Nixon's talks should take place with the Presidents of the Commission and the European Council (Nos. 97 and 101). Similar procedural objections were raised by the French when at a meeting of EC Political Directors on 25 May, their representative resolutely opposed the preparation of a paper on EC/US relations for a ministerial meeting on 5 June: such a report, the French claimed, 'would amount to putting a finger into the cogwheels of a process that would lead to some kind of collective high-level response to the Kissinger speech ... and would thus amount to playing the American game of "globalisation"' (Nos. 102-104).

Kissinger persisted in denying that the United States was, by emphasising the inter-relationship of various transatlantic issues, trying to blackmail the Europeans in the economic field. Rather, he reasoned, it was because it was impossible for the two sides of the Atlantic to emphasise regional egoism in economics, while maintaining the doctrine of integrated defence within the NATO structure. The United States wished 'to lift the debate out of the rut of purely technical controversies'. It was not a case the French were ready to endorse. Nevertheless, during talks with Nixon in Reykjavik during 31 May-1 June Pompidou appeared to adopt a more accommodating stance. According to the American record of their conversations, the two Presidents concurred that the study and development of the concept of the 'Year of Europe' should be pursued 'through both bilateral and multilateral exchanges, carried out simultaneously and at high levels'; that discussions should be held in the NATO context in the forthcoming ministerial meeting in Copenhagen; and that a meeting at Deputy Foreign Minister level might be desirable to evaluate the results of consultations 'with a view to the possible formulation of a Declaration of Principles' (No. 106). It subsequently emerged, however, that Pompidou did not feel himself committed to such a detailed programme (No. 115). At a political cooperation meeting of EC Foreign Ministers on 5 June Jobert indicated that he was ready to participate in a European search for a common response to the Americans, though he made it plain that France was not in favour of any 'new multilateral European/American machinery' (No. 110). For their part, British officials found it difficult to gauge French intentions. Jobert was in no hurry to begin preparing a joint European position, and his Political Director, François Puaux, emphasised that the French felt that they alone were ready to resist American demands, and that they were therefore in a 'mood of withdrawal' on the question of a common European foreign policy (No. 114).

FCO officials were equally perplexed by Kissinger's secretive methods, particularly his preference for confining discussions to a very narrow circle. During talks in Washington on 4 June he warned Trend, despite previous assurances to the contrary, that unless the Europeans did something quickly Congress would legislate for the withdrawal of some 75-95,000 US troops from Europe. He also rejected a suggestion from Cromer that the French should be inspired to draft a transatlantic declaration of principles. He was, he said, opposed to giving them 'a veto over what might be the last chance (as far as the US was concerned) to anchor the Atlantic relationship' (No.

108). Yet, following a meeting with Jobert on 8 June, Kissinger reported that the French Foreign Minister had agreed to consider an *ad hoc* multilateral meeting of Deputy Foreign Ministers, and had offered to draft a section of the projected declaration. Neither of these assurances was ever confirmed by the French (Nos. 117 and 135). Nor was any French draft forthcoming. Indeed, the European response to Kissinger's initiative was disparate to say the least. Nonetheless, by June the EC was ready to address Washington's commercial grievances, dollar devaluation seemed likely to lead to an improvement in America's balance of payments, and, although French opposition diminished prospects of a broad-based US/European declaration, there remained the possibility that something could be achieved in NATO. Oliver Wright, the DUS responsible for superintending the FCO's European Integration Department, suggested that the obvious way of offering the Americans satisfaction might be in NATO communiqué to be issued after Nixon's European visit. 'Could not NATO', he asked, 'get down to drafting a splendid Communiqué—a poem in praise of beauty, truth and goodness in transatlantic defence relations?' If Kissinger still continued to demand his 'ball of wax', his exercise would be revealed 'less as an honest attempt to put more sex appeal into the transatlantic relationship and more as a bit of private enterprise on his part to add the European scalp to his Russian and Chinese trophies, and so improve his own position in Washington' (No. 113). As, however, Cromer explained to Greenhill in a telegram of 11 June, there was a danger that a Europe unsympathetic to American concerns might provoke Congress to 'say to hell with all foreigners'. In his opinion Kissinger feared that traditional links in trade, money and defence 'might well atrophy unless [a] positive and active effort [were] made to avoid this' (No. 120).

Clearly, the American initiative could not be ignored, especially as on 14 June Cromer received 'in strictest confidence' from the White House a brief, but all-embracing, list of subject headings for a projected Declaration of Principles (Nos. 123-24). Nevertheless, the problems facing the adoption of a single declaration covering security, and monetary and trade questions, were, FCO officials concluded, 'insuperable', and they would have to 'think in terms of more than one Declaration, with a different pattern of European countries subscribing to them' (No. 130). In any event, as Heath reminded his Cabinet colleagues on 20 June, only five months after Community enlargement the Europeans were not ready for a unified approach to the Americans, and found unacceptable the way in which Washington had launched the 'Year of Europe' without prior consultation with them. There was though little sympathy in London for the rather negative attitude of the French. Some in the Cabinet felt that it might be in Britain's interests to take a tougher line with a government which seemed to have two objectives in the EC: 'to retain the net advantage which they enjoyed from membership of the Community and to use their growing economic strength to establish themselves as the dominant force in Europe'. If, however, it was argued that Britain's 'overriding concern was to preserve the association of the United States in the defence of Europe', it was also accepted that Anglo-French cooperation was 'basic to the success of the Community' and that Britain should not seek to precipitate a major confrontation with France (No. 137). Meanwhile, the FCO prepared draft declarations for use in NATO and EC/US contexts, though in the words of Michael Butler, Head of the European Integration Department, there was no disposition on the Cabinet's part to 'take the lead in trying to pull Dr Kissinger's chestnuts out of the fire' (Nos. 144).

British diplomats were also inclined to believe that Nixon needed some kind of transatlantic declaration to sell his European policy to an increasingly isolationist and protectionist Congress. 'I cannot see advantage', Overton observed, 'in resisting the idea of a Declaration if the White House want it, the more so if, from the European point of view, it largely consists of hot air. From the US point of view, hot air is an important aid to locomotion' (No. 151). Nor apparently could Douglas-Home. But he had to reckon with a French Government which appeared ambivalent both in respect of policy and procedure. During a meeting with Nixon and Kissinger at San Clemente in late June Jobert was handed two draft declarations of principles, one the work of the State Department and another emanating from the National Security Council (NSC), both of which covered a wide range of subjects and were evidently intended to embrace EC and NATO members, and both of which were subsequently communicated to Cromer. According to what Kissinger told Cromer, Jobert then reaffirmed his intention to draft a section on the 'European role in the Atlantic concept', and 'expressed the hope the British and Germans would likewise work on drafts'. They should all consult bilaterally, and the French would then be ready to consider a deputy Foreign Ministers' meeting (No. 145). However, when during talks with Jobert on 2 July Douglas-Home suggested that a declaration might take the form of two communiqués, one after Nixon's visit to NATO and the other after his visit to the EC, Jobert replied that the French Government 'were not at all sure that they wanted a document or documents'. He also remarked that France 'was very cautious about moving towards a European position, because it thought that other members of the Community, and in particular the Germans, would accept the American document as it was'. And when Douglas-Home expressed the hope that the EC Commission should join the Foreign Ministers of the Nine in trying to construct some document as a basis for discussions with the United States, Jobert insisted that the French Government wished to keep political cooperation clearly separated from the business of the Council of Ministers, and that if other governments sought to push France too far in this matter it would not hesitate to absent itself from the discussions (No. 146).

Meanwhile, Cromer found Kissinger 'sour and tetchy', and evidently irritated at the absence of any constructive response to his 'Year of Europe' proposals (No. 150). In a personal message to Heath of 18 July Nixon wrote that he was 'more than ever impressed with the need and the urgency of putting Atlantic relations on a firmer basis' (No. 160). Yet on the European side there remained a basic contradiction between those who, like the Germans, were ready to make verbal and even material concessions to the Americans to ensure their continued involvement in Europe (Nos. 157 and 165), and at the other extreme the French, who believed the Americans to be in Europe to serve their own interests and therefore in no need of special consideration (No. 166). The British, for their part, set great store by the forthcoming meeting of the Foreign Ministers of the Nine at Copenhagen on 23 July. It was hoped that this would break the existing procedural impasse, and that it would then be possible to inform Washington that they had begun a process which 'should enable them to make a coherent and positive response' when Nixon visited Europe in the autumn (No. 164). Only limited progress was, however, made at Copenhagen. While Jobert accepted that work should begin on a paper establishing Europe's identity *vis-à-vis* the United States and the preparation before the next ministerial meeting on 10/11 September of a report dealing with subjects which could be taken up in a Euro-American dialogue, he sought to delay consideration of other transatlantic issues, especially those concerning Nixon's projected European visit (Nos. 167-70). Moreover, in a brief exchange with Sir Michael Palliser, Britain's Permanent Representative to the EC, he went on to accuse the British Government of failing to keep its Community partners informed of its dealings with Washington regarding the communication of the proposed declarations (No. 171).

This, Douglas-Home noted, was 'nonsense' (*ibid.*). But Heath's reference in a message to Nixon of 26 July to the French 'exploiting' Britain's 'failure' to keep its partners informed of its bilateral transactions with the United States was clearly resented in Washington (No. 174). In his reply of 27 July Nixon pointed out that the US Government would have preferred to use multilateral channels, but had accepted bilateral talks because it agreed with the British view that the French should not be isolated. 'If', he observed, 'we have sought to preserve the privacy of our bilateral exchanges it was largely at European request and because we agreed that under the circumstances it was the best way to make progress.' Nixon was also disappointed by Heath's assessment of the Copenhagen meeting. In view of the Nine's continued preoccupation with procedure, he thought it unlikely that Europe and the United States could 'devise the extraordinary forum that would be appropriate for this important endeavour', and he doubted the wisdom of his attending meetings within NATO and with Community Foreign Ministers if these did not 'yield concrete results and occur in a spirit and at a level commensurate with the urgent need of the times' (No. 178). Kissinger delivered an even more critical verdict on recent developments when he met once more with Trend and Brimelow in Washington on 30 July. He was irritated by the tardy response of the Europeans, and upset at the prospect of the US Government having to receive from the Foreign Minister of Denmark, the country then holding

14

the EC Presidency, a draft declaration resulting from consultations amongst the Nine in which the United States would not have been involved. The Danish Foreign Minister would, he protested, be no more than a 'messenger boy'. Had the Americans known that the *'Year of Europe* would develop into an adversary relationship', they would not, he said, 'have embarked on the exercise' (No. 179).

Kissinger was, however, particularly annoyed at what he depicted as disloyalty on Britain's part. He had expected to work with the British 'in a spirit of mutual confidence', yet they had chosen to discuss with other Europeans a draft declaration which would not be presented in Washington until September. 'It was', he objected, 'a new development in US relations with Britain. Never before had there been a failure at the beginning of a major negotiation to keep each other informed of their thinking.' He added that he was not going to take further initiatives: that whether or not Nixon went to Europe would depend on the procedure and the substance of the Nine's proposals; and that Nixon would certainly not sign any communiqué with anyone below his rank (*ibid.*). Heath attributed much of this to Kissinger's inadequate preparation, imperfect understanding of the situation in Europe, and secretiveness of manner. American rancour derived from Kissinger's failure to make more of his initiative and Nixon's domestic difficulties. In a message he sent from Ottawa, where he was attending a Commonwealth Heads of Government conference, to Brandt and Pompidou on 3 August, Heath observed: 'Unless and until the United States Administration recognises the nature of the Community and the extent to which we all feel bound to reach a Community decision before getting into detailed discussions with the US, and the complex institutional factors involved, we shall not achieve better understanding.' But while Heath thought there was a good deal of bluffing on the American side, he also recognised that Congressional pressures could lead to substantial US force cuts in Europe. He therefore urged on Brandt and Pompidou the need for a European initiative, and to this end he suggested that they should meet with him in Paris at the end of August or in early September for informal discussions in preparation for the next Copenhagen meeting of EC Foreign Ministers (Nos. 181-82).

Both the French and German leaders responded cautiously to this idea. Brandt shared Heath's concern over the future of transatlantic relations, but, anticipating difficulties with the French, suggested that before any ministerial meeting senior British and German officials should make a coordinated approach to Jobert (No. 188). And while Pompidou did not reject the idea of a tripartite summit, he emphasised in his reply that all nine EC member-states must be involved in defining Europe's attitude towards the United States, and he questioned the wisdom of giving a 'visible, solemn and to a certain extent spectacular character to the preparation of the exchanges of views' on EC/US relations (No. 189). Neither Pompidou nor Jobert was, in the opinion of Christopher Ewart-Biggs, Britain's Minister in Paris, 'sorry to see the American Year of

Europe bogged down' (No. 190). British officials nonetheless persisted with their preparation of a draft declaration of principles for submission to representatives at Brussels of NATO's EC member-states. This, in focusing upon transatlantic cooperation in the defence and security spheres, asserted that the independence of Western Europe was 'as vital to the security and prosperity of the North American members of the Alliance as [was] the support of these members to the defence of Western Europe'. It also referred to the allies seeking 'to eliminate conflict in their international economic policies' and encouraging mutual 'economic collaboration'. In addition, on 8 August the FCO despatched two texts to Copenhagen: (1) a draft EC/US communiqué or declaration for issue at the end of a presidential visit; and (2) a paper containing British ideas on how Europe's identity might be defined in relation to the United States. The former foresaw continuing EC/US cooperation in such fields as the promotion of freer trade and international monetary reform, while the latter proposed that the Nine assert 'their own purposes and interests in a way which [did] not require, though it [might] receive, American endorsement' (Nos. 192-93).

The prospects for securing French acceptance of the sort of EC/US declaration the British had in mind did not in the first instance seem particularly bright. Ewart-Biggs, who well understood the problem of trying to relate on paper 'what America [was] to what Europe [was] hoping to be', feared that the French would regard the British draft as 'too much directed to common purposes and values', and 'too much like the Americans want[ed]' (No. 201). The most, he predicted, they were likely to accept were EC/US and NATO texts which would be more in the nature of the necessary communiqués which would accompany a visit from Nixon than 'anything like an Atlantic Charter'. Defence and economics would, he added, have to be kept firmly separate (No. 205). But the British Embassy in Paris maintained steady pressure on the Quai d'Orsay and the Elysée, and during conversations with Heath on 26 August and Brimelow on the 29th Jobert appeared to soften his approach. Evidently disturbed by West Germany's inclination towards adopting a more independent stance in its relations with the United States and the Soviet Union, Jobert agreed with Heath that 'it was vitally important to do everything [they] could to lock the Federal Republic into the European Community and the developing European entity' (Nos. 209 and 211). Jobert also acknowledged the importance of the Copenhagen meeting, and on 28 August Puaux indicated to Ewart-Biggs that an EC/US declaration on the lines proposed by the British might provide a basis for discussion, and that the French could contemplate a NATO declaration at the conclusion of Nixon's visit (No. 210). Two days later, at a meeting of the recently-established EC Correspondants' Group at Copenhagen, a consensus emerged that the British draft EC/US declaration would be a 'good basis for a drafting exercise'. The French nevertheless remained sticky over procedural points, both with regard to a European summit meeting with Nixon and any preparatory talks with the Americans (No. 213). 'They are', Ewart-Biggs observed, '... pathologically sensitive about any implication that Europe is in any sense subordinate to or dependent upon the United States. It is strangely like a sort of Third World psychosis towards the colonial power' No. 210).

Heath was for his part only too anxious to reassure Washington about developments in Europe. In a personal message of 4 September he informed Nixon that all Britain's actions had been 'directed simply and solely to trying to help Europe to agree on some formulation of its position which [would] be intended not in any sense to confront [the President] with a fait accompli but to provide the basis of a lasting relationship between the United States and Europe' (No. 217). Moreover, the British had grounds for optimism. Douglas-Home was much encouraged by the news from Copenhagen that on 5 September EC Political Directors had made further progress towards agreeing a draft EC/US declaration that might be recommended to Ministers. The resulting draft inevitably involved more emphasis on reaffirming what was, rather than breaking new ground, and was rather less than the Americans might have hoped for, but, as Douglas-Home explained to Cromer, it represented a considerable achievement on Britain's part in persuading its EC partners, 'particularly the French', to accept the 'principle that there should be a collective response to the Americans and that declarations should be produced' (Nos. 219-22). The ministerial meeting on 10/11 September also proved satisfactory from the British point of view: there was a large measure of agreement on the preparation of a European identity paper; a revised list of questions to be discussed with the Americans was agreed; and it was decided that the draft EC/US declaration would be completed by the Correspondants' Group for delivery to the Americans on 19 September. 'The European end of the transatlantic dialogue, on which the Nine are now ready to embark, will not', Douglas-Home observed, 'be managed as tidily as we might prefer, but it will be managed' (Nos. 226-27).

Unfortunately, from the British point of view, the American end was not. The US Administration was evidently unhappy about procedures which appeared to exclude it from a say in the in the initial drafting of the projected declaration, and with the dilatory response of the Europeans to a gesture which, according to Kissinger, was intended to answer their fears about a US/Soviet condominium and the possible withdrawal of US forces from Europe (Nos. 228-29). During a conversation with Douglas-Home in New York on 24 September Kissinger, who had just succeeded William Rogers as Secretary of State, again complained about Britain's role in the affair. 'Britain', he said, 'had never been treated as a foreign government', Washington 'had not expected to have to take so literally the concept that Europe as a unit should respond' to the US initiative, but now found itself confronted with a *fait accompli* in the form of a draft declaration. With regard to the prospect of having to negotiate with the Danish Foreign Minister, as the representative of the Community, Kissinger observed that

America was 'in danger of losing her traditional contacts in return for not the most qualified of interlocutors' (No. 232). Subsequent talks between the Political Committee of the Nine and US representatives in New York nonetheless proved friendly and non-adversarial. The Americans found the substance of the EC draft 'thin', and they wanted more emphasis to be given to the changes they saw in the nature of the transatlantic relationship and a firmer commitment to 'partnership' and consultation between Europe and the United States. Yet, as Oliver Wright pointed out in a telegram of 29 September, it was encouraging that the Americans seemed to have to come to terms with the emerging unity of the Nine and that they were ready to work on the European draft, and that the French appeared to accept that the 'exercise must proceed to eventual success' (Nos. 235-38).

Cromer was less optimistic. The US Administration was preoccupied with the consequences of the Watergate affair and the opening of a criminal investigation into the conduct of the Vice-President, Spiro Agnew, and it seemed increasingly unlikely that Nixon would be able to visit Europe before the end of the year. In a letter of 2 October, Cromer warned Brimelow that 'logic and calm discussion [were] at something of a discount' in Washington, and that it would be advisable to go for 'a satisfactory if not on all counts ideal declaration'. It would, he observed, 'be a mistake to allow ourselves and our European partners to be lulled into a sense of euphoria or false security by the progress which has undoubtedly been made over the past week or so' (No. 239). Officials in London were fully alive to the advantages of securing an early agreement. Their general aim was to achieve a common position amongst the Nine for the next round of discussions with the US scheduled for 18 October. That was unlikely to be easy, and the French remained the 'main problem', especially as some of the proposed American amendments seemed likely to confirm their original doubts about the whole exercise. The French disliked the idea of Europe being committed to formal 'partnership' with the United States, and they would almost certainly oppose the commitment implicit in another of the American amendments to the establishment of new transatlantic institutions (Nos. 240-41). But Puaux, who visited London for a meeting with Oliver Wright on 8 October, proved more constructive than expected, even conceding that the French 'had been pleasantly surprised to find that, far from being a Trojan Horse, British views had proved this summer to be very "European"' (No. 254). The FCO also drew encouragement from the tabling of a French draft NATO declaration in Brussels, which the Americans accepted as a basis for future negotiations (No. 257). Moreover, the meetings in Copenhagen on 18-19 October of the Political Directors of the Nine, and between these and representatives of the EC Commission and the United States, went better than expected. According to Wright, the atmosphere was 'easy and friendly' and remaining differences were discussed 'without anything in the nature of an adversary relationship developing' (Nos. 307-08).

Wright thought the Americans deserved some credit for the success of the Copenhagen talks. Helmut Sonnenfeldt of the National Security Council and Walter Stoessel, Assistant Secretary for European Affairs in the State Department, were ready to accept the Nine's rejection of both the 'ball of wax' approach and American efforts to institutionalise the EC/US relationship. 'The unity of the Nine', Wright noted, 'has clearly impressed them and the progress of the exercise has educated them in the mysteries of the Community and all its works.' Even the French seemed ready to adopt a more conciliatory approach, with Puaux emerging as a convert to political cooperation. If the Nine could continue to achieve common positions, which the United States regarded as reasonable and constructive, and if they could increasingly deal collectively with the United States, this, noted a Guidance telegram of 15 October, 'should result in a healthier and more equal relationship' (No. 291). But Douglas-Home was inclined to blame Kissinger, his personal diplomacy and 'furtive secrecy', for much that had gone wrong. He had insisted on conducting the whole complex exercise from the White House and, Douglas-Home complained, had denied himself the use of officials more experienced in the conduct of inter-allied relations (No. 302). Moreover, the future of the EC/US declaration was far from settled, and no date was arranged for the next meeting between the Nine and the Americans. This, it was assumed, would depend on developments in the EC and the timing of Nixon's visit to Europe, and that in turn seemed likely to depend on the outcome of Watergate and, more ominously, events in the Middle East. Indeed, by mid-October the 'Year of Europe' seemed very much a secondary international issue when compared with the battles then being fought in Sinai and on the Golan Heights, and the prospective consequences for Western economies of a doubling in the price of oil and the decision of Arab states to cut back on its production and supply. A long predicted shortfall in global energy resources became truly an energy crisis.

Predicting crisis and promoting peace

Amongst the several commitments which Kissinger volunteered on America's part in his 'Year of Europe' speech was a readiness to 'work cooperatively [with Europe] on new common problems'. In this context Kissinger mentioned specifically 'energy' and 'the challenging issues of assurance of supply, impact of oil revenues on international currency stability, the nature of common political and strategic interests and long-range relations of oil-consuming to oil-producing countries'. 'This', he added, 'could be an area of competition: it should be an area of collaboration' (No. 70). There was little that was new in this. The continued availability of affordable supplies of fossil fuels and the growing dependence of Western industrialised nations on the relatively under-developed oil-producing states of the Middle East, had for some time been matters of concern to officials in Whitehall. They had to reckon both with an ever-expanding world demand for oil, and with an increased readiness on the part of producer-states to flex their economic and political muscle. The Organisation of Petroleum Exporting Countries (OPEC) readily exploited its enhanced bargaining position in negotiations with the major oil companies over host state participation in their operations and price rises to compensate for dollar devaluation. Meanwhile, company interests were further challenged by the moves of radical Arab régimes in Libya and Iraq to nationalise oil production. The governments of producer-states seemed set on gaining ownership of their indigenous oil reserves, thereby facilitating direct deals between consumer- and producer-states and stimulating unregulated competition for available Middle Eastern supplies. While this could benefit the United States and Japan, it would almost certainly be to Britain's detriment, particularly insofar as it would probably weaken British Petroleum (BP) and Royal Dutch Shell, companies in the first of which HMG had a controlling interest, and in the second of which British investors had a 40% stake. Britain was, however, fortunate in having substantial reserves of coal and natural gas, and it was predicted that by 1980 off-shore oil fields in the North Sea would account for about half of its petroleum requirements. Indeed, the Government's determination to maximise the benefits of Britain's raw materials to the national economy, and its reluctance to share its assets with its European neighbours, were to complicate both the development of an EC energy policy (No. 58) and other measures, such as those stipulated by the Organisation for Economic Cooperation and Development (OECD), designed to achieve greater international cooperation in the event of a major crisis arising over oil supplies.

The twin issues of Britain's adherence to long-standing arrangements for pooling oil supplies in Europe in the event of an emergency, and Britain's relations with other consumer-state governments and the big oil companies in the light of changes in the world oil scene, were subjected to interdepartmental scrutiny during August-December 1972 by the Cabinet's Oil Policy Committee. Composed of officials representing the FCO, the Department of Trade and Industry (DTI) and the Treasury, and chaired by John Liverman of the DTI, the committee recommended in its final report of 1 January 1973 that, while HMG should keep its options open with regard to the emergency pooling of oil supplies, it must in cooperation with other consumer-state governments play a more active role in negotiations between the oil companies and producer-states. But the committee expressed a preference for 'arrangements which [were] not too institutionalised' (No. 23), and doubts were expressed about an idea floated by the Central Policy Review Staff (CPRS) for the establishment of an Organisation of Petroleum Importing Countries (OPIC) to balance OPEC's power (Nos. 5-6). Such a body, it was feared, would increase the risk of confrontation with the oil producers and involve the international regulation of British oil companies. Instead, the committee favoured an FCO proposal aimed at avoiding damaging competition amongst major oil consumers. This foresaw the negotiation of an agreement between EC members, the United States and Japan undertaking that none of them would enter into any bilateral arrangements with oil-producing countries, or permit their national oil companies to do so, which would be detrimental to other signatories (No. 23). It seemed, however, inevitable that in future governments were going to have to play a greater role in negotiating with producer-states, and at a meeting of Permanent Under-Secretaries on 24 January 1973, called to discuss the briefing of the Prime Minister for his forthcoming visit to Washington, there was general acceptance of the need for some kind of body to protect oil consumers from producer 'blackmail'. 'The maximum political leverage open to the consumer countries', it was suggested, 'lay perhaps in the threat to withdraw diplomatic and military support from the Governments of the producer countries and leave them to the mercy of the Russians. If they screwed the oil companies too hard on terms, we should do no worse—and might do better—buying from Eastern European Governments than from Middle Eastern ones' (No. 16). Likewise in Washington, the Administration stressed the need for some kind of consumer action, and Kissinger even appeared keen on the idea of US/Japanese collaboration in the development of Soviet oil fields (No. 21).

On 11 April the Cabinet's Ministerial Committee on Economic Strategy endorsed the Oil Policy Committee's conclusions, predicating further decisions on the contents of Nixon's forthcoming energy message and proposals from the EC Commission on the Community's future energy policy (No. 64). However, Nixon's Special Message to Congress on Energy Policy of 18 April dwelt mainly on measures for conserving and further exploiting America's own resources, and neither the EC nor the OECD were able to agree on any immediate action. In any event, as Greenhill observed in a minute of 26 April, covering a Planning Committee paper on EC relations with Middle East oil producers, consumer cooperation, political coordination and a joint effort on aid and credits were praiseworthy, but 'at best palliatives'. These would 'not prevent a grave problem emerging by 1980' when Britain, even with its North Sea reserves, would, according to current estimates, be importing 25% of its oil from the Middle East. Arab producers, operating in a near monopoly environment, would meanwhile encourage prices to spiral with worrying financial consequences (No. 74). They would also be able to cut supplies on commercial or political grounds, and might employ their 'oil weapon' in the hope of securing the solution they wanted to the still simmering Arab-Israeli dispute. During the Six Day War of 1967 Israeli forces had overrun all the territory of the former Palestine mandate, and had since remained in occupation of the Sinai peninsula in Egypt and Syria's Golan Heights. It was a situation which was anything but stable, and which, despite the mediatory efforts of Gunnar Jarring, the UN Special Envoy to the Middle East, seemed far from resolution. Egypt and Israel's other contiguous neighbours were not ready to enter into negotiations until the Israelis gave some indication of their readiness to withdraw, and the Israelis made that conditional on the outcome of negotiations (No. 55). Meanwhile, escalating terrorist and counter-terrorist violence seemed destined to lead to a further round of hostilities in the region which could prove catastrophic for Western Europe's oil supplies. With this in mind, the British sought both to improve their relations with the Arab world and to persuade the Americans to use their influence with the Israelis in order to break the prevailing diplomatic deadlock and open the way to negotiations (Nos. 57 and 63).

The British Government had already made its position clear on what it thought should be the basis of a future peace settlement. In a speech, delivered in Harrogate on 31 October 1970, Douglas-Home had reaffirmed British support for United Nations (UN) Security Council Resolution 242, which called for the withdrawal of Israeli forces from territories occupied in 1967, an end to the current state of belligerency, and the recognition of each state in the area's 'right to live in peace within secure and recognised boundaries'. He had further explained in detail that this should involve recognition of the frontier between Israel and Egypt as it had existed prior to the war, that that between Israel and Jordan should be based on the pre-war armistice lines, subject to minor changes, and that once Syria had accepted Resolution 242 the same principles should govern its boundary with Israel.[9] In spirit these ideas resembled the plan put forward by William Rogers, the then US Secretary of State, in a speech on 9 December 1969 calling for the withdrawal of Israeli forces to the pre-war armistice lines. Yet these proposals, which the Israelis had rejected, were not ones to which Cromer thought the Americans likely to return. For the moment, the Americans seemed more interested in facilitating 'proximity talks' aimed at achieving an interim agreement between Egypt and Israel in Sinai—an arrangement which had little appeal to the Egyptians, who were unlikely to achieve thereby more than a partial withdrawal of Israeli forces. As, however, Cromer acknowledged in a despatch of 17 April, Nixon would not try to compel Israel to make concessions. He was inhibited by domestic political constraints and by the belief that such pressure would be ineffective, and Cromer thought that, while America's growing dependence on imported oil might move Nixon 'to make a fresh attempt to grasp the Middle East nettle', the threatened energy crisis would not alter very much the strict limits within which US policy had to be formulated. '[T]he Administration' Cromer surmised, 'are likely to conclude that Middle East stability and American access to Arab oil are most likely to be preserved by continuing to keep Israel in a position of such strength and confidence that the Arabs are effectively deterred from initiating large scale military action against her' (No. 66).

The Americans may, as Cromer noted, have assessed a full-scale Arab-Israeli war 'as on the whole unlikely' (*ibid.*). But on 1 May Egypt's President, Colonel Mohamed Anwar al-Sadat, delivered a powerful and bellicose speech which, though it stopped well short of promising war,

[9] Lord Home, *The Way the Wind Blows* (London: Collins, 1976), pp. 296-301.

announced a new stage of 'total confrontation' in a struggle against American and Israeli efforts to reinforce the territorial *status quo* (Nos. 82-83). There was, evidently a good deal of posturing in this, and in conversation with Douglas-Home, Kissinger continued to argue that 'the strongest leverage on the Arabs was the danger of another crushing defeat' (No. 89). For their part, the British could at least draw some satisfaction from the fact that Sadat expressed his gratitude to Britain and France for their recent support for the Arab cause in the UN Security Council. Resolutions 331 and 332, carried respectively on 20 and 21 April, called for a thorough review of the Middle Eastern situation and condemned Israel's recent attacks on Lebanon. This raised the prospect of the Security Council considering the Middle East as a whole for the first time since November 1967 and, as Anthony Parsons, the AUS responsible for superintending the FCO's Near East and North Africa Department (NENAD), explained in a letter of 27 April, with all other options apparently closed, 'the forthcoming debate could now offer an opportunity, however slight, to make a serious attempt to break the deadlock'. The 'main tactical objectives' of the Security Council meeting should, Parsons thought, be to bring the Arabs closer to some kind of negotiating process, and the Israelis closer to declaring themselves on boundaries, in the hope of achieving the 'main strategic objective' of an 'ongoing process of negotiations' (No. 80). It could also buy time for Sadat until after the forthcoming Israeli general elections when the moment might be more propitious for negotiations.

The Americans were altogether more sceptical about the possibility of the Security Council producing any constructive result. The Israelis were likely to oppose the establishment of any form of UN machinery for handling the situation and, in the words of Joseph Sisco, US Assistant Secretary of State for the Middle East and South Asia, there was a risk that the Security Council meeting 'would contribute to fostering the Egyptian illusion that someone else [would] relieve them of the necessity for the painful decisions needed if there [was] ever to be a negotiation' (Nos. 91-93). Indeed, according to John Moberly, Counsellor in the British Embassy in Washington, the State Department appeared to think that time was on the side of eventual negotiations, and the White House was preoccupied with domestic affairs and the failure of the cease-fire to hold in South-East Asia. 'This', Moberly observed, 'probably means that short of an outbreak of fighting on the Suez Canal front, we shall have to wait at least until after the Israeli elections and probably until 1974 for any concerted American diplomatic moves to break the deadlock' (No. 99). The Israelis likewise felt that little good could come of the Security Council debate. Abba Eban, Israel's Foreign Minister, thought that the Egyptians regarded the Security Council as 'a substitute for negotiations not as a prelude to them', and on 22 May he assured Douglas-Home that there were 'no real military preparations in hand' in Egypt and that the 'chances of Sadat doing something irrational were no more than 3%' (No. 100). Heath found it depressing that Eban showed no sign of understanding the dangers facing Israel and its neighbours. But he was even more disturbed by the prospect of the Arabs applying their oil weapon. 'As a result of the energy crisis and the growing effectiveness of OPEC', he minuted on 4 June, 'it is now within the Arabs' power to withhold oil supplies from the Americans, and perhaps from Europe as well, unless the United States and others cease to furnish any political or military support to Israel' (No. 109).

Douglas-Home shared Heath's concerns. Yet, as he pointed out to the Prime Minister in a minute of 7 June the existing deadlock in the Middle East could not be broken except by the United States, the only country that could exert the necessary leverage on Israel, and he was not sure that the Americans saw a settlement as desirable in itself. The danger of a global super-power confrontation had receded with détente, and a settlement would, in reducing Arab dependence on the West, allow Arab 'turbulence' to reassert itself. Personally, however, Douglas-Home feared that in the absence of a settlement the Arabs would become 'more frustrated, radicalised and irrational', and that there would be a growing danger of the interruption of oil supplies for political reasons and of the Arabs trying to use their financial power to damage Western economies. Meanwhile, he recommended that Britain seek to protect its position in the region by: (1) supporting the Arabs in the UN; (2) multiplying economic links and 'being as generous as possible with aid to the important Arab have-nots', notably Egypt; (3) selling the Arabs such arms as they wanted, so long as this did not conflict with the policy of supplying no weapons which might increase the chances of a resumption of fighting; and (4) continuing to develop a common Middle East attitude in the EC. He also suggested that Heath write to Nixon urging the United States to use its influence to induce the Israelis to adopt a more conciliatory approach towards the Arabs (No. 112). In the resulting message, sent on 15 June, Heath pointed to the 'threat of an energy crisis', the increased dependence of the West on Arab oil, and the problems associated with the movements of vast oil revenues. 'All the signs are', he observed, 'that this situation is going to get worse, not better, and that unless we can do something about the Arab/Israel problem our whole industrial power and progress may be threatened' (No. 127).

If the Americans were perturbed about the possible Arab use of the oil weapon, they seemed determined not to show it. In conversation with Parsons in Tehran on 11 June Rogers recalled that he had told the Arabs that there was no question of the United States 'being held to ransom', and that the Americans would be ready to take the necessary conservation measures and to develop alternative energy sources if the Arabs were unready to sell their oil at bearable prices (No. 122). Nixon had, however, referred to US involvement in international efforts, particularly with the OECD, to explore long-term energy problems and the prospects for an agreement for sharing oil in times of acute shortages. The matter came up again during talks between British and US officials in London on 11 June. Julius Katz, Deputy Assistant Secretary for Economic and Business Affairs in the State Department, then stressed that the United States would not favour a consumer cartel or the creation of some special organisation. The Americans, he said, could not offer a 'dramatic approach to the problem', but they were in favour of more frequent consultation bilaterally, in groups, or within the OECD. As Oliver Wright added, it was easier to state the problem than to provide the answers. 'Unless consumers cooperated', he remarked, 'there would be a free-for-all situation but we were all reluctant to set up a cooperative mechanism' (No. 118). EC Ministers had so far failed to agree on a common European approach to the energy problem, and while within the Cabinet and the FCO it was generally accepted that consumer cooperation was the only way of avoiding a competitive scramble for oil supplies, there was also a desire that Britain should not appear to be the promoter of an anti-OPEC cartel. Indeed, by the end of June Parsons, who personally did not rate highly the risk of serious hostilities, had concluded that Britain might best follow the line of France, Italy and Japan on consumer-producer cooperation, though the price the producers would ask 'would be a sympathetic attitude to the Arab view of the Israel problem' (Nos. 138, 143 and 154).

There was in the meantime no indication that the Americans thought there was any need for urgent action in the Middle East (No. 139). During his visit to the United States in mid-June the Soviet leader, Leonid Brezhnev, expressed his concern to Nixon over what, in the absence of an Arab-Israeli settlement, might happen in the coming months. But while Nixon subsequently assured Heath that he had had the Prime Minister's earlier comments on the Middle East 'in mind', his response to Brezhnev was singularly non-committal (No. 141). The UN Security Council debate on the Middle East, which began on 6 June and adjourned on the 15th, left British diplomats with hardly more grounds for optimism (No. 125). British efforts to persuade the Americans to take the Council meeting seriously and to make a genuine attempt to use it to start a fresh negotiating process ended in failure. The British had hoped that through contact between the Americans and the Egyptians it might be possible to agree language for a consensus in the resumed Security Council debate on 20 July (No. 148). The Egyptians were determined, however, to have a resolution, and the Americans opposed anything that went further than reaffirming Resolution 242. And on 26 July a draft resolution submitted by India and seven other non-permanent members of the Council, expressing serious concern about Israel's lack of cooperation with UN peace efforts and its continued occupation of conquered territories, received thirteen votes, including that of the United Kingdom, but was vetoed by the United States (No. 175). As Parsons noted, the last few days of the debate were 'rather agonising and the outcome was indeed unsatisfactory'. Particularly distressing from the British point of view was the American attitude. 'The Americans', he added, 'like the Israelis, seem to have regarded the whole Security Council meeting as anathema from the outset and to have decided from an early stage that there was no hope of their being able to associate themselves with any outcome; or rather that any agreed outcome would make life more difficult for them' (No. 177).

The failure of the Arabs to make any headway in the Security Council stimulated further talk of their resorting to the 'oil weapon'. King Feisal of Saudi Arabia was said to be 'seething about the American veto', particularly as he had previously encouraged Sadat to believe that he, Feisal, might be able to influence the Americans towards a more moderate Middle Eastern policy, and it was confidently predicted that he would soon announce a levelling off of Saudi oil production at its current rate (No. 187). The Americans were, indeed, dubbed a 'political liability' by Greenhill when in September he and other officials returned to discussing the subject of consumer cooperation and oil supplies. Nevertheless, in a despatch of 7 September Sir Philip Adams, Britain's Ambassador in Cairo, argued that although Sadat had tried every stratagem short of war in his endeavour to secure the return of Sinai to Egypt, he did not believe that the President now shared the views of those who saw war as the only solution to Egypt's problems. 'He', Adams continued, 'impresses me personally as a man of peace and I am sure he knows that further war with Israel at the present time would not only ruin Egypt but make his own position intolerable' (No. 224). Likewise, reports from Israel seemed to suggest that the Israelis were becoming more amenable to negotiations with the Arabs. On 24 September Eban remarked to William Ledwidge, the British Ambassador to Israel, that while there was no immediate threat to peace, if a negotiating process could be started 'it would reduce the risk of any Arab leader being so unwise as to break the ceasefire out of sheer frustration' (No. 233). And despite reports in early October that the Syrians were redeploying their armed forces and the Egyptians were engaged in large-scale military exercises, the Israelis seemed confident that for the time being their neighbours were set on keeping the peace. On 4 October an Israeli military spokesman reckoned that there was no more than a 2% chance of the Syrians engaging in offensive action, and only after reports reached Tel Aviv that the Soviet Union had been evacuating personnel from Egypt were Israeli forces partially mobilised (No. 242 and 244). Colonel Reuter, an Israeli military spokesman, told the British Defence Attaché in Tel Aviv on the morning of 6 October that the moment might be 'propitious' for an Arab resort to force (No. 246). But, beyond this, neither British diplomats in the Middle East nor the FCO in London appear to have had any premonition of the news, telegraphed that afternoon from Tel Aviv, that Egyptian and Syrian forces were attacking Israeli positions in Sinai and on the Golan Heights (No. 247).

The fourth Arab-Israeli War

The differing British and American perceptions of the situation in the Middle East were clearly revealed in their reactions to the outbreak of the fourth Arab-Israeli war. Kissinger's immediate response was to seek support for a UN Security Council resolution calling for a cease-fire and a return to the *status quo ante* (No. 249). The American military appreciation was that the Arab armies would soon be in retreat and Kissinger considered it essential to prevent the situation deteriorating to the point of a confrontation between the super-powers in support of their local clients. Once begun, proceedings in the Security Council would be allowed to follow at a 'stately pace' (No. 253). Much, however, to his irritation, he found the British reluctant to back a resolution calling on the Arabs to withdraw from territory over which the British considered the Egyptians and Syrians to retain sovereignty. HMG's preference was for a resolution which would re-affirm Resolution 242, call for a cease-fire, and require the UN Secretary-General to promote a negotiated settlement (No. 250). In a paper setting out British objectives in the crisis Parsons argued that Britain had little leverage on either the belligerents or the Americans and that any initiatives it might take might well prove fruitless. 'We must', he noted, 'therefore avoid saying or doing things which are unlikely to produce results and which will serve only to alienate the Arabs, thus increasing the risk to our oil supplies.' This meant avoiding any association with the Israeli war effort or apparently pro-Israeli American policies, and standing firm on the 'Harrogate position' (No. 259).

The FCO also had a clear idea of what would be the most promising outcome of the conflict. It would, according to Parsons, be one in which the situation on the Golan Heights was stabilised, Jordan and the Lebanon were not involved in the war, and the Egyptians were left holding positions on the east bank of the Suez Canal. This could mean that the Arabs would feel that their military and psychological posture had improved to the point where they could engage in serious negotiations, while the Israelis, having extinguished the Syrian threat to their security, '*might* feel disposed to be more flexible regarding a settlement with Egypt'. The 'psychological moment' might come when the Egyptians felt unable to hold their gains in Sinai and the Israelis might be wondering whether they could afford the hard slog to drive the Egyptians back (*ibid.*). British diplomats were, however, doubtful about whether that moment had yet arrived when on 12 October Kissinger asked Cromer if Britain would consider putting forward a cease-fire *in situ* resolution in the Security Council. Kissinger revealed that Anatoly Dobrynin, the Soviet Ambassador in Washington, had informed him on the 11th that the Egyptians would acquiesce in such a move. The United States could not, he said, put forward such a resolution 'because of its own Jewish constituency' and, like the Soviet Union, it would abstain from voting. He further suggested that the resolution be tabled on 13 October when Congress would not be in session (Nos. 267, 269 and 272). Heath and Douglas-Home agreed that no opportunity should be missed for securing a cease-fire if the 'psychological moment' was right, but information already received from Cairo and Tel Aviv indicated that while the Egyptians would only be interested in such a cease-fire if it were clearly linked to a total Israeli withdrawal to the 1967 lines, the Israelis would be looking to trade their military gains made on the Golan for their losses in Sinai (No. 270).

Subsequent British enquiries in Cairo confirmed that insofar as the Egyptians were concerned this was indeed the case (No. 272). Sadat, who dubbed the proposed British initiative a 'Kissinger trick', maintained that he could only accept a cease-fire 'which was directly linked to a final settlement' (No. 274). He also made it clear that he would have the support of China and that the Chinese would veto the projected Security Council resolution (No. 279). Kissinger was, however, adamant that he had Soviet assurances that Egypt would accept a cease-fire *in situ*, and during a telephone conversation on 13 October he put 'extreme pressure' on Douglas-Home to act as he requested (No. 276). If no resolution were introduced on the lines he proposed, the Americans, he warned Cromer, 'would pour in arms supplies to Israel and see what the battle brought forth' (No. 277). Douglas-Home was, in principle, ready to make a move in the Security Council (hopefully with the French), 'if such a move would be likely to make things better not worse' (No. 275). Yet, as Cromer was well aware, Kissinger was putting Britain in a 'very awkward position', asking it to act as an 'American stalking-horse with the Arabs' and to bear the risk of Arab unpopularity if the Russians were deliberately leading the West astray (No. 278). This too was the view taken by Ministers and senior officials at Chequers on the evening of the 13th, and soon afterwards Douglas-Home telephoned Kissinger to inform him that HMG did not think the time 'ripe for this initiative' (Nos. 280-81).

This decision exposed Cromer to a fresh onslaught from Kissinger. Summoned to Kissinger's presence, he was told that Nixon 'could not recall any crisis in the last three years when the British had been with the Americans when the chips were down'. The US Administration was, admittedly, in a difficult position. The Israelis, having suffered a serious military setback in Sinai, were critically short of ammunition, and there was growing pressure in Congress for some response to the resupply operations of the Russians. Moreover, Kissinger was inclined to see the Arab-Israeli conflict in terms of East-West relations, and to view Egyptian successes as a reverse for American influence in the Middle East. Yet, as Cromer reminded Kissinger with regard to the massive resupply of Israel that he was planning, 'Europe would not be content to go without Middle East oil because of American actions' (No. 282). The current assessment in London was that, if the fighting did not last more than ten days and Britain took no action to antagonise the Arabs, there should be no serious threat to UK oil supplies. If, however, the Israelis gained too much of an advantage, or Jordan were drawn into the war, Britain could face the total disruption of supplies of Arab oil in an attempt to force the West to put pressure on Israel. Arab oil accounted for 65-70% of Britain's supplies, and it had stocks equivalent to 75 days' consumption and the equivalent of 21 days' consumption in transit. As John Hunt, Trend's successor as Cabinet Secretary, pointed out in a minute of 9 October, this suggested avoiding action which 'would provoke the Arabs to turn off the tap' (No. 256). The producer-countries were already demanding the effective doubling of posted oil prices (No. 266) and on 16 October, following news of the American emergency supply of arms to Israel, EC representatives in Jedda received from the Saudi Arabian Foreign Ministry a warning that if the Nine did not 'bring pressure to bear on the Americans to adopt a more even-handed policy in the Arab/Israel dispute, Saudi Arabia would cut back her oil production' (No. 296). The next day the Organisation of Arab Petroleum Exporting Countries (OAPEC), then meeting in Kuwait, announced that member-states would be reducing their oil production by 5% each month until the Israelis had withdrawn from the occupied territories 'and the legal rights of the Palestinian people were restored'. Moreover, while the OAPEC communiqué stated that these measures should not harm any friendly state which actively and materially assisted the Arab cause, it was evident that Western Europe's dependence on Arab oil made it far more vulnerable than America to such production cuts (No. 304).

HMG had meanwhile to reckon with growing public concern over the effects on Israel of the embargo Britain had imposed at the commencement of hostilities on arms supplies to the battle-field states. Douglas-Home informed the Cabinet on 16 October that Britain could well sacrifice its ability to influence peace moves and Arab policy on oil if it were to reverse its decision on the embargo (No. 298). For similar reasons the Americans were denied the use of British bases for their resupply operation (Nos. 287 and 297). Yet, in truth, the prospects for a cease-fire were more likely to be affected by decisions taken in Washington and Moscow than in London, and the Americans seemed far more worried by Soviet 'adventurism' in the Middle East than by the threat posed to European economies by the denial of Arab oil. Donald Rumsfeld, the US Permanent Representative to NATO, told the North Atlantic Council on 16 October that it had to be made clear to the Russians that détente was a two-way street (Nos. 299-300). Three days later, on the 19th, he explained that the American view was that the Alliance should not be concerned with the search for a peace formula, but should concentrate upon dissuading the Warsaw Pact countries from aggravating the situation (No. 309). The Israelis had by then managed to establish a bridgehead on the west bank of the Suez Canal and, worried lest the Russians should be tempted into some military intervention to prevent an Egyptian debacle, Kissinger travelled to Moscow on the evening of 19 October evidently in the hope of winning Soviet support for an *in situ* cease-fire (No. 311). Cromer thought Kissinger's fears of the Russians being 'tempted into some rash act of military intervention' exaggerated. 'But', he observed, 'embarrassed super-powers bemused as to how to attain their goals with their clients rampant in an orgy of success or defeat can only leave us with concern as to what they might do' (No. 315).

Kissinger's Moscow visit resulted in a US/Soviet agreement to sponsor a UN Security Council resolution calling for a cease-fire within twelve hours of its adoption, implementation of Resolution 242, and negotiations aimed at establishing a just and durable peace (No. 318-19). These provisions were incorporated in Security Council Resolution 338 of 22 October, and both Egypt and Israel subsequently accepted the cease-fire. But when later that day, during a brief stopover in London, Kissinger discussed these matters with Douglas-Home, he admitted that he had 'given no thought to machinery for observing the cease-fire' and that he expected the American and Soviet airlift of arms to continue. Kissinger also indicated that no specific negotiating machinery had been worked out, that he was not thinking of a peace conference on Vietnam lines, and that he expected the Arabs and Israelis to talk directly to each other with the Americans and the Russians only present at crucial stages. 'As you will see', Douglas-Home telegraphed Cromer, 'there are an alarming number of loose ends and a great lack of precision about machinery for peace-making and peace-keeping.' Kissinger's inclination to keep all but the superpowers out of the act did not bode well for the future and, as Douglas-Home predicted, was likely to cause difficulties with the French and others who would be determined to get in on the act (No. 321). This was only too apparent when, following further fighting in Sinai and the advance of Israeli forces to Suez on 23 October, the US and Soviet representatives on the Security Council pushed ahead with a further resolution calling for a return of the combatants to the positions they occupied when the cease-fire became effective, and for the despatch of UN observers to supervise its observance (No. 331).

Other members of the Security Council were evidently irritated by the failure of the super-powers to consult fully with them. Even more alarming, however, was the failure of the resolution to bring a halt to the fighting. With their 3rd Army surrounded by Israeli forces at the southern end of the Canal, the Egyptians appealed for American and Soviet forces to be sent to the war zone. The Americans turned down the request (*ibid.*). The US Government was opposed to introducing contingents of either super-power into the Middle East in anything but a truce supervisory role. But during the early hours of 25 October Kissinger telephoned Cromer to inform him that Nixon had just received a personal message from Brezhnev saying that if the United States did not join in sending forces to intercede in the cease-fire, the Russians might have no choice but to act unilaterally. The United States, Kissinger stated, were 'not immediately informing their NATO allies', but were 'going onto a low level of military alert including cancelling of leave to affected naval and military in the neighbourhood of hostilities' (No. 329). As Kissinger subsequently explained, the US Government was aware that some seven or eight Soviet airborne divisions were on alert and that a Soviet flotilla was heading for Egypt. It was not, however, until noon on the 25th, by which time Brussels was abuzz with press rumours of the American alert, that Rumsfeld formally informed the North Atlantic Council of Washington's decision (No. 371). Rumsfeld's statement helped clear the air. Nonetheless, Sir

Edward Peck, Britain's Permanent Representative to NATO, reported that discussion of the press reports prior to the announcement had been 'somewhat acrid' particularly since, as the Chairman of the Military Committee had indicated, 'although US alert measures were purely national, SACEUR [Supreme Allied Commander, Europe] might wish to take corresponding alert measures with other national forces under his command' (No. 332).

America's unilateral military action did little to inspire confidence amongst its allies. The British were already perturbed by Kissinger's tough talk, his refusal to be 'blackmailed by the Arabs', and his apparent failure to comprehend the problems faced by Western Europe as a result of cuts in their oil supplies (Nos. 321 and 324). 'It seems to me', Cromer wrote in a telegram of 23 October, 'that the whole cohesion of the Atlantic Alliance could be put in jeopardy if the Arab world is not satisfied with the equity of the eventual outcome of the military conflict, and consequently vents its frustration by withholding oil from Europe' (No. 322). Kissinger was not slow, however, in expressing his own disillusionment with the attitude of European governments towards the Middle Eastern crisis. When on the evening of 24 October Cromer had tackled him on the dangers to allied unity of an oil embargo, he had replied that he was beginning to draw 'melancholy conclusions about the cohesiveness of the Alliance', adding: 'It never cohered on anything except the one thing least likely to arise: a military attack on Western Europe.' Moreover, while Kissinger insisted that he was 'doing everything possible to get the maniacs to stop fighting', he explained to Cromer that the essential first step would be a US initiative aimed at persuading the Arabs to call off their oil embargo, and that only then would Washington work out with the Arabs a negotiating strategy to be implemented after the Israeli elections on 11 December. Pressure on Israel before then would, he maintained, play into the hands of the right-wing opposition and make the problem more intractable (No. 328). This was a time-table for negotiations which in Cromer's view appeared 'likely to lead inevitably to the taking up of fixed positions of the kind which [had] bedevilled all attempts in recent years to get negotiations going' (No. 336).

Brezhnev's warning, nonetheless, seemed to reinforce the need for greater urgency. Douglas-Home was not surprised by its content: he had long believed that the Russians would not accept another Arab humiliation. If there were to be any chance of the situation calming down then, he informed Cromer, it would be necessary: (1) to despatch to the sensitive battle-field area as many truce observers as could be mustered; (2) to begin the negotiations envisaged in Resolution 338 within the next two or three days; and (3) to achieve an understanding which would end the plight of Egypt's beleaguered 3rd Army. The latter, he suggested, might be secured by a deal unrelated to fundamental issues, such as an immediate exchange of prisoners and the lifting of the Egyptian blockade of the Bab el-Mandeb in exchange for a withdrawal of Israeli forces sufficient to 'to let the

Egyptian force off the hook' (No. 330). Security Council Resolution 340 of 25 October, which decided on the establishment of a UN Emergency Force from which, on American insistence, the troops of permanent members were excluded, went some way towards defusing current tensions. And Douglas-Home hoped that the very seriousness of the situation might increase the possibility of finding a solution to the whole Arab-Israeli problem. In a draft message to Nixon of 31 October Heath argued that the situation would 'almost certainly go sour' unless negotiations were started rapidly and unless some progress could be seen on the ground towards the implementation of Resolution 242. Otherwise, he feared that the Russians would be able to strengthen their position by rebuilding the Arabs' military strength, and that there would be a progressive tightening of the oil screw as well as attacks on other Western interests in the area. 'We should then', Heath added, 'be faced by a stronger Soviet power base in the Middle East, accompanied by a massive economic decline of the European allies of the United States.' He also urged that such negotiations take place under the auspices of the UN Secretary-General, with the United States and the Soviet Union offering their good offices to the parties. Conscious of French objections to the super-powers trying to settle matters over the heads of the UN Security Council, he contended that such procedures would avoid giving offence to other countries with interests in the region and the results might look less like an imposed solution (No. 350).

Kissinger had no objection to the presence of Kurt Waldheim, the UN Secretary-General, at the talks. While, however, he hoped for Security Council endorsement of US/Soviet arrangements for the negotiations, he was opposed to its direct participation in them. Evidently frustrated with the attitude assumed by America's European allies towards the war, and particularly the difficulties which had arisen over the supply and refuelling of US aircraft, he yet again took Cromer to task for Europe's jeopardising the Alliance. On 31 October he protested 'that it was impossible to point to one constructive act by Europe in the context of European/US relations [that] year' (No. 352). Some US diplomats took a rather more relaxed view of transatlantic relations. Stoessel for one was of the opinion that the relationship was based on 'enduring common interests', though Oliver Wright found it necessary to remind him that the NATO alliance had specific aims and that the crisis in the Middle East had to a large extent been outside them. American and European perspectives in the region were not the same. 'Europe', Wright observed, 'was both nearer to the Middle-East and much more dependent on it for oil supplies' (No. 354) But EC member-states were neither at one in their responses to the war, nor uniformly affected by Arab oil diplomacy. In the latter respect Britain was more fortunate than some of its neighbours. Three of the principal oil producing countries, Saudi Arabia, Abu Dhabi and, less precisely, Qatar, had offered HMG assurances that they had no wish to damage Britain and that they would take steps within their power to prevent that happening. Other states had received no such assurances (No. 353). Indeed, the

Netherlands, whose public stance had seemed more sympathetic to Israel than the Arabs, was faced with an embargo on approximately 58% of its oil imports (Nos. 347-48). This presented the FCO with a problem of extreme delicacy. If the British were to assist their allies and partners they risked being accused by the Arabs of thwarting their intentions and might then have to face the prospect of the extension of the embargo to themselves. On the other hand, a refusal to allow the re-export of oil to friendly states, especially in the EC, raised practical difficulties and could be in breach of the Treaty of Rome (No. 356).

James Cable, head of the FCO's Planning Staff, summed-up the dilemma faced by the British policy-makers in a minute of 2 November. It would, he there argued, hardly serve British interests 'if, with Transatlantic and Anglo-American relations under strain, we then find that the European alternative has crumbled when confronted with its first major challenge' (No. 360). During a visit to London William Casey, US Under-Secretary of State for Economic Affairs, also insisted that in the absence of effective consumer cooperation, the Arabs would be encouraged to think that they could pick off the Community countries one by one and that 'their oil weapon was more successful than they otherwise expected' (No. 376). Yet, British thinking was that the best way to help the Netherlands was to work for a joint position of the EC countries, in the hope that the Dutch would not be worse treated by the Arabs and, at best, their supply position might be improved (Nos. 365, 372 and 378). At a European Council meeting on 6 November British and French Ministers agreed, with broad support from the Irish and the Italians, that 'the key issue was to ensure the continued flow of crude oil to Western Europe' and that, despite Dutch and German wishes to the contrary, the best way to ensure that was to say as little as possible about European consumer solidarity (No. 377). The Council, evidently with a view to encouraging an early settlement of the Middle Eastern conflict, also issued a declaration urging a return of Arab and Israeli forces to the positions held on 22 October, expressing the hope that peace negotiations begin within the 'framework of the United Nations', and recalling that the UN Charter had entrusted to the Security Council the principal responsibility for international peace. A future peace agreement, it stated, should be based on the need for Israel to end the territorial occupation it had maintained since 1967, respect for the sovereignty, territorial integrity and independence of every state in the area and their right to live in peace within secure and recognised boundaries, and recognition that a just and lasting peace must take account of the legitimate rights of the Palestinians (No. 375).

The declaration provided Britain and France with what John Davies, the Chancellor of the Duchy of Lancaster and effective Minister for Europe, described as 'a firm Community position on which to base their efforts to persuade the Arab states to moderate their embargo on oil supplies to Holland' (No. 383). It was, however, hardly calculated to appeal to Americans, many of whom, both within and without the Administration, were shocked by the rift that had occurred between the United States and its allies over the Arab-Israeli war and by the readiness of the Europeans to 'give in to "Arab oil blackmail"' (No. 396-97). Kissinger regarded the declaration as a 'gesture to the Arabs' which cut across his own peace efforts and, in conversation with Carrington on 7 November, James Schlesinger, the US Secretary of Defense, complained of a British tendency 'to work in close collusion with the French' and of British policies 'taking on the quality of "decayed Gaullism"' (No. 379). But 'close collusion' did not always translate into close cooperation. The French were distinctly cautious about a British proposal to link the declaration with a joint EC démarche to Arab governments aimed at dissuading them from continuing to make progressive over-all cuts in production and bringing home to them the dangers of discriminating between Community members (Nos. 385-86 and 388). Apparently irritated by the action of the Danes, the Dutch and the Irish in voting in the UN General Assembly against French nuclear testing and reluctant to expend their credit in Arab capitals for disloyal partners in Europe, the French delayed agreement on the proposed démarche until 21 November (Nos. 393, 400-403 and 424). For the moment, however, this was as far as the British themselves were prepared to go in the interests of European solidarity. They were in favour of medium- and long-term collaboration within the EC on energy matters, but as Stephen Egerton, Head of the Office's Energy Department, noted in a minute of 29 November, 'we must resist short term collective or collaborative approaches which would either set at risk our supplies from the Arab world, or prejudice our full employment at a later stage of the benefits of North Sea Oil' (No. 423).

The Energy Crisis and the End of the Year of Europe

Kissinger meanwhile succeeded in winning Egyptian and Israeli agreement to a six-point cease-fire package (No. 413). He nonetheless returned from a tour of Middle Eastern capitals disappointed by his failure to persuade Arab leaders to relax their oil embargo. He had impressed on the Saudi King that he would 'not be willing to pay the domestic price of bringing pressure to bear on Israel while being subjected to Arab blackmail' (No. 210). Yet, as Cromer observed in a telegram of 22 November, hints of American retaliation against the Arab oil-producing countries seemed 'unlikely to be conducive either to an easing of the oil embargoes or to progress in the peace negotiations', and they could be 'potentially disruptive in the NATO setting'. Hardly less disturbing was Kissinger's reversion to public criticism of his European allies. At a press conference on the 21st he complained, in a remark which was readily assumed to be directed at Britain, that those countries which had been most consulted by the United States had 'proved among the most difficult in their co-operation' (No. 404). Then in conversation with Cromer on 24 November, Kissinger, after expressing his indignation at a proposed EC/Japanese bilateral declaration, protested that the 'special relationship was collapsing' and that, while Britain's entry into the EC should have raised Europe to the level of Britain, it had in fact reduced Britain to the level of Europe. It was 'tragic', he said, that the EC/US declaration, which he had conceived as a cooperative gesture, had 'led to the establishment of an adversary relationship'. And in response to Cromer's rehearsing of the difficulties Britain had encountered with the French in drafting, he objected that he could not see how the French could always stand out against the British and the Germans. The British, he claimed, were no longer acting as a counter-weight to the French, who 'were now being allowed to dominate European thinking on the Atlantic relationship ... and were seeking to build up Europe on an anti-American basis'. This, he characterised, as 'the worst decision since the Greek city states confronted Alexander' (No. 412).

Douglas-Home was spurred by Kissinger's language into drafting a 'frank and fairly robust reply'. In a personal message to Kissinger of 28 November he again explained Britain's stance on the Arab-Israeli conflict, his long-held belief that peace in the Middle East required an Israeli withdrawal from the occupied territories, and his regret that he had previously failed to persuade the Americans to press the Israelis to work to this end. He also repeated that Britain was firmly alongside the United States on East-West issues, but that Washington must take its allies more into its confidence and consult with them during the period of build up towards crisis and confrontation. And while he admitted that the Nine's response to Kissinger's 'Year of Europe' initiative may have seemed 'almost culpably slow', he reminded Kissinger that it had caught the Europeans 'on the hop' and when the Community's machinery for rapid response 'simply wasn't there'. The fact that Kissinger was due to visit Brussels and London in December also offered the prospect of private talks with British and other European leaders (Nos. 420-21). Indeed, Douglas-Home was inclined to believe that a 'fence-building exercise on the part of the Nine collectively could be advantageous' and to this end favoured the idea, initially floated by the Americans, of discussions between Kissinger and the Foreign Ministers of the Nine in the margin of a forthcoming NATO ministerial meeting (Nos. 405 and 416). Oliver Wright even speculated whether by then it might not be possible to have the draft EC/US declaration ready for completion. Colleagues thought that unlikely given that many matters still remained to be settled (Nos. 407 and 414). But Jobert appears to have been opposed to any other kind of discussion between Kissinger and the Nine, fearing what Puaux called 'political cooperation à dix'. The French, Tomkins observed in a letter to Brimelow, 'are in a sensitive mood', suspecting the British of forcing them to adopt positions which would put them into a minority of one in the Community (Nos. 425-26).

The French reaction towards this British proposal exemplified the differences between Britain and France in their attitude towards the United States and transatlantic relations. 'In short', Tomkins observed in a letter to Brimelow of 30 November, 'we are both agreed that there should be a distinct European personality vis-à-vis the Americans, but we want this personality to have a close and satisfactory dialogue, and they want it to behave like a young woman anxious to preserve her virginity from the GIs' (*ibid.*) Thus thrust between the new Alexander and a coy virgin, Sir Alec was left with little room for manœuvre. He was, however, determined to press ahead with the completion of the European identity exercise, and an FCO paper which he submitted to the Cabinet's Ministerial Committee on European Strategy on 23 November recommended 'rapid progress towards a common foreign policy', albeit linked to progress on other Community policy fronts (No. 406). The identity paper, the final version of which Butler despatched to Washington on 7 December, hardly seemed likely to offer any offence to the Americans: it recognised Western Europe's dependence on the Americans for its defence, emphasised the close ties binding the two sides of the Atlantic, and declared the Nine's intention 'to maintain their constructive dialogue and to develop their co-operation with the United States on the basis of equality and in a spirit of friendship'. Yet, on 29 November *The New York Times* reported that the Nine were 'secretly' drafting this paper for issue at their forthcoming summit and that US officials, who had seen parts of the draft, 'were commenting wryly that the US call for a new Atlantic Charter had produced a new European Charter instead' (No. 428). It was doubtless accounts such as this that Cromer had in mind when in a telegram of 2 December, which he devoted to analysing the steady deterioration of transatlantic relations since 1972, he argued that Europe, and particularly Britain, needed 'to be more frank in its dealings with the United States on Community affairs' (No. 432).

Unfortunately, from the European point of view, Kissinger seemed automatically to consider almost anything that the Nine might attempt independently of the United States as evidence of a potentially adversary relationship (No. 433). And Kissinger's own diplomatic method, the fact that he so often stressed the need for greater transatlantic consultation, but put little effort into consulting with America's allies on anything but a bilateral basis, did little to reassure the French. The Americans may have thought they were doing the Europeans a favour by launching the 'Year of Europe'. Yet, as Cromer noted, it 'was typical that they should omit to discover in advance if it was the sort of favour Europe wanted' (No. 432). Kissinger denied this charge: he had, he told the NATO ministerial meeting in Brussels on 10 December, gained the impression from the several European leaders he had consulted before 23 April that they would welcome his speech. However, he protested, since then 'discussions between the United States and the Nine had been enmeshed in legalistic disputes over language that had ended up repeating and deepening the very concerns that the Americans had sought to satisfy'. He also complained that the present practices of the Nine made consultation 'pretty meaningless', adding those 'who negotiated would not speak while those who spoke could not negotiate' (No. 447). The next day, in discussion with the Foreign Ministers of the Nine, Kissinger won broad support for the idea of substituting a 'shorter and more eloquent [EC/US] declaration' for the current draft, which he evidently considered 'too legalistic and journalistic'. But possibly the most constructive contribution to the ministerial debate at Brussels was that made by Douglas-Home when he suggested at a private NATO meeting that members should use the Alliance's 25th anniversary to restate old truths (Nos. 449-50). Out of this eventually emerged the NATO summit of June 1974 and the Ottawa Declaration reaffirming the fundamental principles of the Alliance.[10]

During his meeting with NATO Ministers on 10 December Kissinger emphasised the need for a common effort towards solving the energy crisis. 'The United States', he said, 'could solve its energy problems only with great difficulty, Europe could not solve them at all' (No. 447). The point was well made, but Western governments were still far from united in their attitude towards the oil producers. A Joint Intelligence Committee report of 5 December, which speculated on the possibility of US military intervention in the Middle East to secure oil supplies, concluded that 'even without any serious upsurge of popular anti-Americanism in Europe, the Nine would probably be unable to agree on any strong pro-American line, particularly one that would involve the use of force; the French, in particular, would be unwilling to associate themselves with the Americans' (No. 434). The Europeans were in any case still divided amongst themselves. EC ministerial meetings on 3-4 December seemed simply to paper over cracks, with the Dutch complaining of the reluctance of the British and French to back concrete measures to deal with the oil embargo, and the Germans threatening progress on such matters of particular interest to Britain as the establishment of a Regional Development Fund (RDF) (No. 435). British officials continued to believe that if the Arab states saw that their oil embargo was being openly frustrated, this would provoke them to reduce oil supplies further, and that in these circumstances it was essential to continue to resist public declarations of European solidarity. This would, according to an FCO telegram to Bonn of 10 December, be better pursued in the political field, including: participation in the search for a Middle Eastern settlement; efforts to persuade the Arabs to remove their discriminatory embargo on the Netherlands; and 'driving home the point that they [would] not advance their political purpose by inflicting hardship on their friends' (No. 445-46). The French seemed even more resolutely opposed to statements of consumer solidarity. In a conversation with Douglas-Home on 11 December Jobert affirmed that France, while ready to work for consumer-producer cooperation, 'would not associate itself with any declaration restricted to the consumers alone' (No. 448).

This did not augur well for the initiative which Kissinger launched the following day in London. On 12 December, in an address to the Pilgrims' Society of Great Britain, he proposed that Europe, North America and Japan should join in establishing an Energy Action Group of senior and

[10] Cmnd 6932, *Selected Documents Relating to Problems of Security and Cooperation in Europe, 1954-77* (London: HMSO, 1977), pp. 184-86.

prestigious individuals with a mandate to develop within three months an initial action programme for collaboration in all areas of the energy problem. Producer-nations were to be 'given an incentive to increase supply', and were to be invited to join the group 'from the very beginning with respect to any matters of common interest'. Douglas-Home welcomed the speech as a 'positive timely and statesmanlike initiative' (Nos. 457-58). And if DTI officials thought Kissinger's proposals 'somewhat half-baked', particularly insofar as they failed to tackle the problem of how a consumer scramble for oil was to be avoided, they too favoured a positive response (No. 462). Aware that the idea of an Energy Action Group had been conceived primarily as a catalyst for mobilising the resources of consumer-countries, and that it therefore risked the possibility of a confrontation with producer-countries, British diplomats nevertheless felt that in the medium and the longer terms if offered scope for consumer-producer cooperation (Nos. 456 and 470). They were also worried lest the French should block progress on the proposal on the grounds that the EC must first elaborate its own energy policy, and that, as in the case of the 'Year of Europe' initiative, this would in turn exasperate the Americans, perhaps leading them to conclude that the Community was incapable of acting as an effective partner (Nos. 460-61). To this end they sought West German assistance (*ibid.*), and an EC summit meeting in Copenhagen on 14/15 December prepared an energy statement which referred to the need for cooperation with both producers and consumers, thereby leaving the way open for further consideration of Kissinger's proposal. Heath failed, however, to persuade Pompidou to agree to the Community's welcoming Kissinger's proposal for an Energy Action Group (Nos. 466, 477 and 485).

A European Council of Ministers meeting on 18/19 December also proved disappointing, and Douglas-Home responded to German stalling on proposals for a Regional Development Fund by refusing to proceed further with the debate on a European energy policy (Nos. 472-73 and 481). Meanwhile, despite the opening of a Middle Eastern peace conference in Geneva on 21 December (No. 479), the energy situation worsened. On the 23rd the Shah of Iran announced that the six main oil-producing Gulf states would raise the price of oil for export from $5.10 to $11.65 a barrel, effectively quadrupling the October price of oil. This constituted more than just a threat to the balance of payments of individual oil-importing countries: it began, Douglas-Home observed, 'to cast in doubt the capacity of the world economic system to sustain it', and in a personal message to Kissinger of 2 January 1974 he stressed that the projected Energy Action Group could have a 'crucial role' in promoting a thorough discussion between consumers and producers (No. 487). Douglas-Home was likewise keen to assure Washington that he would do what he could to ensure that the Nine did nothing which might prejudice either the group's usefulness or Kissinger's diplomacy at Geneva (Nos. 497 and 507). The Government was already having to cope with widespread industrial unrest, including a coal miners's overtime ban, as a result of its efforts to restrain monetary inflation through a statutory prices and incomes policy, and it now faced a 20% shortfall in Britain's oil supplies. All this underscored the importance of having the Americans actively engaged in trying to find a solution to the several problems associated with the energy crisis. 'These problems', noted an FCO telegram of 24 January, 'cannot be solved without them and, unlike Europe, the United States could if necessary go it alone' (No. 516).

The past year had indeed seen a profound shift in the transatlantic balance of power. At the time of Kissinger's 'Year of Europe' speech, the United States was having to cope with a serious balance of payments problem and the consequences of dollar devaluation, and European governments had been able to ignore or reject such concepts as the 'single ball of wax'. By the beginning of 1974 only America seemed capable of rescuing the European economy from the impact of the energy crisis. British diplomats were certainly moving towards the conclusion that the world's energy problems required some degree of consumer cooperation since competitive bilateral oil deals, of the kind in which France appeared ready to engage, must drive fuel prices higher, and that it was therefore imperative to devise a framework for consultation between all states able to influence the situation. Moreover, in political terms no Western country other than the United States had sufficient influence in the Middle East, particularly over Israel, to deliver a peace settlement (No. 496). In economic terms the United States was in a relatively stronger position than Europe when it came to attracting the surplus funds of oil-producing countries and it would have a major role to play in recycling them; and in energy terms the Americans were more self-sufficient than the Europeans. In addition, there remained the danger that America might lose all confidence in establishing a better working relationship with its allies and retreat into protectionism and neo-isolationist policies. Cromer, in his valedictory despatch of 15 January, could still write of an America which was lonely and more uncertain of its place in the world than at any time since 1945. 'The shortest era of Empire in the history of any great nation', he observed, 'is clearly at an end: it was not a role that was deliberately sought, nor comfortably worn' (No. 506). In British eyes, there were therefore good reasons for responding favourably to an invitation which on 9 January Nixon extended to governments of industrially developed oil-consuming nations to a conference of foreign ministers in Washington aimed at establishing a 'task force' to develop a consumer action programme (No. 494).

The French predictably saw matters in a rather different light. They considered the American proposals confrontational and thought the best way forward was through measures clearly designed to promote consumer-producer cooperation (Nos. 489 and 505). They in any case believed it more appropriate to convene the gathering under the auspices of an existing international body such as the OECD and, with a view to avoiding the institutionalisation of consumer cooperation, they eventually proposed a UN-sponsored energy conference. In the words of Michel Freyche, one of

Pompidou's technical advisers, the American alternative, a meeting of Foreign Ministers at Washington, 'would look like a front of rich consumers preparing a confrontation' (No. 499). British diplomats appreciated French reservations, but doubted their motives. Despite his talk in Brussels of the need for more consultation amongst allies, Kissinger had launched his energy proposal without prior warning. An FCO paper, analysing his recent visit to Europe, argued that for Kissinger the United States, with himself as the exponent of its foreign policy, was 'the centre of the world, wherever he happen[ed] to be, and whatever he [was] doing': others were 'pawns on his chessboard'. And, the paper concluded: 'The more we try to do on the basis of any kind of "special relationship" with the US, the more we risk incurring his special wrath and disappointment' (No. 513). The FCO nevertheless pressed for an early response by Community members to Nixon's latest proposals. 'We believe', Douglas-Home noted in a telegram to Paris of 11 January, 'our aims are very close to those of France, particularly in the need to get maximum international co-operation between consumers and producers on crucial aspects, such as price' (No. 502). The British could also rely on the support of a majority of other member-states, including West Germany which now held the EC Presidency, and at an EC Council meeting on 15 January it was agreed, despite some initial resistance on the part of Jobert, that the Community would accept Nixon's invitation on the understanding that all member-states and the Commission would be represented in the Conference (No. 509). But in a subsequent message to Nixon, Heath emphasised the importance HMG attached to 'the close and early association of producer governments and the less developed consumer countries with the work on the formulation of policy for consumer/producer co-operation' (No. 510). In this respect, at least, Britain's position was not so very far removed from that of France.

The British were also at one with the French in pursuing bilateral oil deals with Middle Eastern governments, and in seeking to explore the idea of establishing an EC framework for industrial cooperation between member-states and oil-producing countries. A Cabinet paper of 18 January, prepared by the DTI in consultation with the FCO and the newly-established Department of Energy, saw this last option as way of promoting greater consumer-producer interdependence and thereby assuring oil supplies and moderating prices (No. 512). Officials of the Cabinet's European Unit were, nevertheless, well aware that the current energy and economic crisis 'called for solutions going much wider than the Community alone', and that there were risks of a 'dangerous confrontation' with the United States if other EC countries aligned themselves with France in opposition to Nixon's recent initiative (No. 515). 'Given the importance of engaging US cooperation on international energy questions, we should', Douglas-Home observed, 'avoid administering a collective European snub to the Americans' (No. 522). He need not have worried. At a European Council meeting on 5 February other Ministers seem to have been unimpressed by Jobert's rehearsal of French objections to the projected conference, and little attention was paid to a French draft Community mandate, which was very negative in its approach and mainly concerned with establishing what should not be done at Washington (No. 534). The mandate finally approved by the Council was, however, far from unambiguous, and left the whole question of the Community's attitude towards conference follow-up action particularly ill-defined. It thus declared that the Conference should not become a permanent body or lead to the institutionalisation of a new forum for international cooperation, restricted to the most industrialised countries and replacing existing organisations, but it left open the possibility of establishing a framework of international cooperation. Moreover, while reserving to the Community freedom of action to decide its own energy policies and its own relations with producer-states, the mandate endorsed continuing cooperation with other consumer-countries (No. 535).

The Conference was, as the FCO's steering brief pointed out, 'likely to polarise between the Americans, who wish[ed] to launch a new crusade, and the French who want[ed] to minimise the role of international consumer co-operation and jealously to guard their own and the Community's freedom of action'. Meanwhile, the Community had adopted an 'intermediate position', and it would clearly 'not be easy to reconcile these three attitudes' (No. 539). For the British the Conference also threatened, in Tomkins's words, to bring 'to a point of uncomfortable focus the central problem of [their] convergences and divergences with the French over the position of Europe vis-à-vis the United States, and over the balance of [their] European and Atlantic connections'. As with the 'Year of Europe' initiative, Jobert opposed any further institutionalisation of the relationship between the United States and the Nine, and seemed to see the energy problem and the conference 'in terms of a kind of French conventional wisdom which [made] distrust of the Americans the measure of European cohesion'. But if Jobert seemed likely to press for a minimalist interpretation of the Community mandate, Pompidou appeared reluctant to risk alienating the Americans altogether. Tomkins still considered the situation could be managed, and that at Washington it should be possible to achieve this without alienating the Americans or letting the French involve Britain in a European failure. 'We diverge', Tomkins wrote of the French in a telegram of 9 February, 'only where French prejudices take them away from reality. It is thus in a sense an exercise ... in trying to save them from themselves' (No. 547).

Tomkins was too optimistic. The Conference, which opened in Washington on 11 February and continued until the 13th, soon ran into difficulties over machinery to co-ordinate follow-up work. Kissinger proposed a programme for negotiations which would begin with the formation of a coordinating group to carry out consultations, leading via another Foreign Ministers' meeting to a conference of oil consumers and producers. This vision was, however, rejected by Jobert. After what

Douglas-Home described as a 'notably graceless intervention' (No. 548) during the first plenary session, he staunchly refused at a subsequent ministerial meeting of the Nine to countenance any suggestion of follow-up arrangements. These, he insisted, would be contrary to what the Community had previously agreed, and he himself had only agreed to participate in the gathering on the explicit understanding that the Community would not accept any kind of standing group to continue the Conference's work. There was, however, a strong feeling among other Europeans that, as an FCO guidance telegram subsequently commented, the French should 'not be allowed to get away with it this time', especially when the issues were 'too big and their procedural objections too petty' (No. 553). Indeed, it soon became apparent that there might be no alternative to accepting that in this instance the Community could not act collectively and that the individual member-states must cooperate with the Americans, the Canadians and the Japanese on a national basis. Much of the subsequent debate was concerned with the drafting of a Conference communiqué, and on 12 February Douglas-Home gave full support to an American text which spelt out in fairly precise terms the concept of continuing consultations, including the establishment of a coordinating group, headed by senior officials. This was a turning point in the Conference. It also placed Britain in direct opposition to France, though Douglas-Home was able to rely on the support of seven other EC partners. Jobert continued to fight a rear-guard action over reference in the draft communiqué to future consultations on follow-up within the OECD. He was, however, finally left isolated in Washington, unable to do anything more than express France's dissent from paragraphs and sub-paragraphs in the communiqué which he had earlier sought to emasculate (Nos. 550-51 and 562). Even at the cost of France's dissociation, other EC members thus endorsed the force of Kissinger's arguments and agreed to the concept of progress in the energy crisis through joint action with America as distinct from separate and private bargains.

The French were naturally aggrieved at the way in which they found themselves isolated at Washington. In their view, they had been betrayed by partners who had failed both to respect the Community mandate and to discern the motives underlying Kissinger's divisive diplomacy. Even if Kissinger had not been out to 'sabotage the Community completely', he had, according to Philippe Cuvillier of the French Embassy in London, 'wanted to reduce it to an American poodle' (No. 552). Admittedly, French anger was not directed solely against Britain. It extended to other partners who had seemed to desert them at Washington, particularly the West Germans, whose Foreign Minister, Walter Scheel, had been Community representative in the Conference (No. 559). Nonetheless, French obduracy had forced the British to choose between French and American policies, and in this instance they had had no hesitation in choosing the latter. 'On the merits of the case', Douglas-Home observed, 'the Americans are right and the French are wrong. The world's energy problems can only be solved by co-operation ... It is accordingly imperative to devise a framework for consultation between all states able to influence the present situation' (No. 553).

In retrospect the Washington Energy Conference seems like a defining moment in Britain's relations with France and its other Community partners. British diplomats had hoped that Community membership would enhance their influence in Washington, and that the evolving mechanisms of political cooperation in Europe would eventually result in a common foreign policy of the Nine. But they had long since recognised that little could be achieved within the Community in opposition to France, and they were equally aware that Britain, through its close links with the United States, risked appearing as a Trojan horse amongst the Nine. It was unfortunate that during Britain's first full year in the Community they had to deal with an administration in Washington that evidently expected more from them in Europe than they could possibly deliver, and a government in Paris which set its Gaullist face resolutely against any transatlantic gesture which might appear to formalise Western Europe's subordination to America. Moreover, while the British may have been closer to the French than to the Americans in the way they viewed war in the Middle East, they were convinced that only the United States had sufficient influence in the region to promote a lasting settlement and sufficient resources to assume an international lead in tackling the energy crisis. The result was a divided Community whose differences were made manifest in Washington. In conversation with Cuvillier on 15 February Oliver Wright, who had been a member of the British delegation at Washington, admitted that there was no denying that the Community had been damaged by this experience. 'Those', he said, 'who argued in Whitehall that British interests were best pursued through the Community would now find their position significantly weakened.' In reply, Cuvillier simply remarked that 'the European identity had been a dream with a short life' (No. 554). Kissinger for his part kept up his opposition to a political identity 'systematically sought in separation from, and frequently in opposition to, the United States', and angered by the Nine's handling of the projected Euro-Arab dialogue, announced that he wanted to look again at the US/Nine declaration in the light of the incompatibility between the intentions it expressed and the recent performance of the Europeans (Nos. 563-66). Meanwhile, on 28 February, a General Election deprived Heath's Government of its majority in Parliament and Douglas-Home was replaced at the FCO by James Callaghan, a Secretary of State who, along with his Labour colleagues, was committed to renegotiating Britain's terms of entry into the Community, and who had little sympathy for such notions as European union. America's 'Year of Europe' might perhaps be better regarded as Britain's year of choice.

KEITH HAMILTON

LIST OF PERSONS

Abramson, Sidney, Under-Secretary, DTI, 1972-81

Acheson, Dean, US Secretary of State, 1949-53

Acland, Antony, PPS to Secretary of State for Foreign and Commonwealth Affairs, 1972-75

Adams, Sir Philip, British Ambassador, Cairo, 1973-75

Agnew, Spiro T, US Vice-President, 1969-73

Ahmed, Mahmoud Samir, Minister, Egyptian Embassy, London, 1968-73

Akins, James E, US Ambassador, Jedda, 1973-75

Aldington, Lord, Chairman, Grindlays Bank Ltd, 1964-76. Former Government Minister and Deputy Chairman of the Conservative Party Organisation

Alexander, Michael O'D B, APS to Secretary of State for Foreign and Commonwealth Affairs, 1972-74

Ali, Field-Marshal Ahmad Ismail, Egyptian Defence Minister, 1972-74

Allen, Sir Douglas, Permanent Secretary, Treasury, 1968-74

Alsop, Stewart, US political columnist

Altes, Frederik Korthals, Netherlands Permanent Representative to the EC

Ameen, Mike M, ARAMCO Vice-President responsible for relations with the Saudi-Arabian Government and Service Director, Washington, 1972-75

Amery, Julian, Minister of State, FCO, 1972-74

Andersen, Knud Berge, Danish Foreign Minister, 1971-73

Andronikof, Constantin, interpreter, French Foreign Ministry

Annenberg, Walter H, US Ambassador, London, 1969-75

Anson, John, Under-Secretary, Cabinet Office, 1972-74

Apel, Hans E, Parliamentary Secretary of State, Federal German Foreign Ministry, 1972-74

Archer, Graham R, First Secretary, NAD, 1972-75

Arculus, Ronald, Head of STD, 1970-73; Minister (Economic), British Embassy, Paris, 1973-77

Armstrong, Robert T, PPS to the Prime Minister, 1970-75

Armstrong, Sir William, Permanent Secretary, CSD, 1968-74

Arnaud, Claude, Deputy Political Director, French Foreign Ministry, 1972-75

Arthur, Sir Geoffrey, DUS, FCO, 1973-75

Assad, Lieut-Gen Hafiz al-, Syrian President, 1971-2000

Atherton, Alfred Leroy, US Deputy Assistant Secretary of State, 1970-74; Assistant Secretary of State, 1974-79

Atiqi, Abdel-Rahman Salim al-, Kuwaiti Minister of Oil Affairs, 1967-75

Bahr, Egon, Minister without Portfolio attached to the Federal German Chancellor's Office, 1972-77

Bailey, Alan, PPS to the Chancellor of the Exchequer, 1971-73

Baker, Stephen, Coordinator of Industrial Advisers to the Departments of Trade and Industry, 1974-78

Balfour-Paul, Hugh G, British Ambassador, Amman, 1972-75

Balladur, Edouard, Assistant Secretary-General to the French Presidency, 1969-74; Secretary-General, 1974

Balniel Lord, Minister of State, FCO, 1972-74

Barber, Anthony, Chancellor of the Exchequer, 1970-74

Barnes, Ernest J W, British Ambassador, The Hague, 1972-77

Barratt, Francis R, Deputy Secretary, Treasury, 1973-82

Bayne, Nicholas P, First Secretary, FCO, 1972-74

Bayülken, Ümit H, Turkish Foreign Minister, 1971-74

Beaumarchais, Jacques Delarue Caron de, French Ambassador, London, 1972-77

Beith, Sir John, British Ambassador to Belgium, 1969-74

Bennett, Jack Franklin, Deputy Under-Secretary for Monetary Affairs, US Treasury Department, 1971-74

Bennsky, George M, Director, Office of Fuels and Energy, US State Department, 1973-74

Bergold, Harry E, US Deputy Assistant Secretary of Defense, 1973-76

Bernard, Daniel, Deputy Secretary-General, French Foreign Ministry, 1971-75

Bettencourt, André, Minister attached to the French Foreign Ministry, 1972-73

Bhutto, Zulfikar Ali, Pakistani Prime Minister, 1973-77

Bierring, Ole, Political Director, Danish Foreign Ministry, 1972-76

Blancard, Jean R E, French Secretary for Energy, 1973-75

Boardman, Thomas G, Minister for Industry, DTI, 1972-74

Boemcke, Eberhard, Federal German Deputy Permanent Representative to the EC

Böker, Aldfons, Minister-Counsellor, Federal German Embassy, London, 1970- 75

Boidevaix, Serge, Director of the Cabinet of the French Foreign Minister, 1973-74

Bombassei Frascani de Vettor, Giorgio, Italian Permanent Representative to the EC, 1967-76

Borga, Giuseppe M, Counsellor, Italian Embassy, London, 1973-78

Boumedienne, Houari, Algerian President, 1965-78

Braithwaite, Rodric Q, Head of EID(E), 1973-75

Brand, Robert A, Minister, US Embassy, London, 1971-74

Brandon, Henry, British journalist; Washington Correspondent and Chief American Correspondent, *The Sunday Times*, 1950-83

Brandt, Willy, Federal German Chancellor, 1969-74

Brant, Colin T, Counsellor (Energy), British Embassy Washington, 1973-78

Bretherton, James R, Principal, DTI, 1970-74

Brezhnev, Leonid I, General Secretary (formerly First Secretary) of CPSU, 1964-82

Bridges, Lord, PS (Overseas Affairs) to the Prime Minister, 1972-75

Brimelow, Sir Thomas, DUS, FCO, 1969-73; PUS, FCO, 1973-75

Brown, L Dean, US Ambassador, Amman, 1970-73

Brown, Sir Max, Secretary (Trade), DTI, 1970-74

Brown, Weir M, US Acting Permanent Representative to OECD, Paris, 1972-74

Brunet, Jean-Pierre, Director of Economic and Financial Affairs, French Foreign Ministry, 1966-73

Brunner, Guido, Head of Planning Staff, Federal German Foreign Ministry, 1972-74

Buckley, James L, US Senator (Republican, New York), 1971-77

Bunker, Ellsworth, US Ambassador-at-Large, 1973-77

Burin des Roziers, Etienne, French Permanent Representative to the EC, 1972-75

Burke, James A, US Congressman (Democrat, Massachusetts), 1963-79

Burns, Arthur F, Chairman of the US Federal Reserve Board, 1970-78

Busch, Rolf, Norwegian Permanent Representative to NATO, 1971-77

Butler, F E Robin, PS (Parliamentary Affairs) to the Prime Minister, 1972-74 and 1974-75

Butler, Michael D, Head of EID, 1972-74

Cable, James E, Head of Planning Staff, FCO, 1971-75

Cabouat, Jean-Pierre, Head of General Affairs, French Foreign Ministry, 1970-75

Caines, John, PPS to the Secretary of State for Trade and Industry, 1972-74

Callaghan, L James, Secretary of State for Foreign and Commonwealth Affairs, 1974-76

Cambridge, Sydney J G, Head of FRD, 1973-77

Campbell, Alan, AUS, FCO, 1972-74

Campbell, Gordon, Secretary of State for Scotland, 1970-74

Carlisle, Brian A, Regional Coordinator, Middle East, and Director, Shell International Petroleum, 1970-74

Carr, Robert, Home Secretary, 1972-74

Carraud, Pierre, French Deputy Permanent Representative to NATO. 1972-75

Carrington, Lord, Secretary of State for Defence, 1970-74; Secretary of State for Energy, 1974

Carver, Field Marshal Sir Michael, Chief of the General Staff, 1971-73; Chief of the Defence Staff, 1973-76

Casey, William J, US Under-Secretary of State for Economic Affairs, 1972-74

Catalano di Melilli, Felice, Italian Permanent Representative to NATO, 1970-79

Chalmers, George B, Head of Oil Department, FCO, 1971-73; Head of SAD, 1973-75

Chandler, Geoffrey, Director, Shell International Petroleum Company, 1971-78

Cheysson, Claude, EC Commissioner for Development Aid, 1973-81

Chivers, Christopher J A, APS to the Chancellor of the Exchequer, 1971-73; Principal, Overseas Finance Group, Treasury, 1973-76

Chorafas, Anghelos, Greek Permanent Representative to NATO, 1972-74

Clercq, Willy De, Belgian Minister of Finance, 1972-73

Clinton-Davis, Stanley C, MP (Labour, Hackney Central), 1970-83

Cloake, John C, Head of TRED, 1973-76

Coles, A John, PS to Lord Balniel, 1972-74

Colley, George Joseph, Minister of Finance, Republic of Ireland, 1970-73

Commines de Marsilly, Guy de, Director for the Levant/North Africa, French Foreign Ministry, 1972-75

Connally, John, US Treasury Secretary, 1971-72; Adviser to the US President, June-July, 1973

Cortazzi, H A Hugh, Minister (Commercial), British Embassy, Washington, 1972-75

Cottrell, Sir Alan, Chief Scientific Adviser to HMG, 1971-74

Courcel, Geoffroy Chodron de, Secretary-General, French Foreign Ministry, 1973-76

Cox, Archibald, US Prosecutor in the Watergate Investigation, 1973

Cradock, Percy, Under-Secretary, Cabinet Office, 1971-75

Craig, Albert J M, Head of NENAD, 1972-75

Cranston, Alan, US Senator (Democrat, California), 1968-91

Cromer, Lord (Rowley), British Ambassador, Washington, 1971-74

Crowe, Brian L, First Secretary British Embassy, Washington, 1968-73; First Secretary, British Embassy, Bonn, 1973-76

Crowe, Sir Colin, UK Permanent Representative to the UN, New York, 1970-73

Cubbon, Brian, Deputy Secretary, Cabinet Office, 1972-75

Custis, Ronald A, PS to Secretary of State for Energy, 1974-75

Cuvillier, Philippe, Minister-Counsellor, French Embassy, London, 1973-75

Daniel, E Clifton, Head of the Washington Bureau, *New York Times*

Davidson, Alan E, Head of Defence Department, FCO, 1972-73

Davies, John E H, Chancellor of the Duchy of Lancaster, 1972-74

Davignon, Etienne, Vicomte, Political Director, Belgian Foreign Ministry, 1969-76

Dawbarn, Simon Yelverton, Head of West African Department, FCO, 1973-75

Dayan, Lt-Gen Moshe, Israeli Minister of Defence, 1969-74

Dean, John W, Counsel to the US President, 1970-73

Debré, Michel, French Foreign Minister, 1968-69; Defence Minister, 1969-73

Denman, G Roy, Deputy Secretary, DTI, 1970-74

De Palma, Samuel, US Assistant Secretary of State for International Organization Affairs, 1969-73

De Winton, Michael Geoffrey, Assistant Solicitor, Law Officers Department, 1969-74

Dobrynin, Anatoly F, Soviet Ambassador, Washington, 1962-86

Donaldson, William H, US Under-Secretary of State for Security Assistance, 1973-74

Dondelinger, Jean, Luxembourg Permanent Representative to the EC

Douglas-Home, Sir Alec, Secretary of State for Foreign and Commonwealth Affairs, 1970-74

Drake, Sir Eric, Chairman of BP, 1969-75

Ducci, Roberto, Director-General for Political Affairs, Italian Foreign Ministry, 1970-75

Dufourq, Bertrand, Deputy Director for Western Europe, French Foreign Ministry, 1972-76

Dulles, John Foster, US Secretary of State, 1953-59

Dunnett, Sir James, PUS, MoD, 1966-74

Dyvig, Peter, First Secretary, Danish Foreign Ministry, 1969-74

Eagleburger, Lawrence Sidney, US Deputy Assistant Secretary of Defense, 1971-72; Acting Assistant Secretary of Defense, 1973; Executive Assistant to the Secretary of Defense, 1973-77; Deputy Assistant to the US President for National Security Operations, 1973

Eban, Abba, Israeli Foreign Minister, 1966-74

Ebel, Robert E, official, Office of Oil and Gas, US Department of the Interior, 1966-74

Eberle, William D, US Government Special Representative for Trade Negotiations, 1971-74

Edgar, William H, Second (later First) Secretary, US Embassy, London, 1972-75

Edinburgh, Prince Philip, Duke of, Prince Consort, 1952-

Eekelen, Willem van, Director for NATO affairs, Netherlands Foreign Ministry, 1971-77

Egerton, Stephen L, First Secretary, British Embassy, Tripoli, 1972-73; Head of Energy Department, FCO, 1973-77

Ehrlichman, John D, Assistant to the US President for Domestic Affairs, 1969-73

Eilts, Hermann F, US Ambassador, Cairo, 1973-79

Elizabeth II, Queen of Great Britain and Northern Ireland, 1952-

Ellingworth, Richard H, Counsellor, British Embassy, Tehran, 1972-75

Elliott, Mark, PS/PUS, FCO, 1973-74

Ellis-Rees, Hugh F, Assistant Secretary, Cabinet Office, 1972-74

Ellsworth, Robert F, US Permanent Representative to NATO, 1969-71; Assistant Secretary for International Security Affairs, US Defense Department, 1974-75

Elslande, Renaat van, Belgian Foreign Minister, 1973-77

Ennals, David H, Minister of State, FCO, 1974-76

Eralp, Orhan, Turkish Permanent Representative to NATO, 1972-76

Ersboell, Niels, Danish Permanent Representative to the EC

Ervin, Samuel J, US Senator (Democrat, N. Carolina), 1954-74; Chairman, Senate Watergate Committee, 1973

Evans, D, Assistant Secretary, Cabinet Office

Evans, Sir Vincent, Legal Adviser, FCO, 1968-76

Ewart-Biggs, Christopher T E, Minister, British Embassy, Paris, 1971-76

Faber, Richard S, Counsellor, British Embassy, The Hague, 1969-73; Counsellor British Embassy, Cairo, 1973-75

Fahd ibn Abdul Aziz, Prince, Saudi Arabian Minister of the Interior, 1962-75; Second Deputy Prime Minister, 1967-75. Succeeded his brother, Khalid, as King, 1982

Fahmy, Ismail, Egyptian Ambassador, Bonn, 1972-73; Minister of Tourism, April-October 1973; Foreign Minister, 1973-77

Fargue, Jean, Second (later First) Secretary, French Embassy, London, 1972-75

Feisel (Faisal) bin Abdul Aziz, King of Saudi Arabia, 1964-75

Fenn, Nicholas M, Assistant Head, Science and Technology Department, FCO, 1972-74

Fenton, Roy Pentelow, Chief, Overseas Department, Bank of England, 1965-75

FitzGerald, Garet, Republic of Ireland Foreign Minister, 1973-77

FitzHerbert, Giles H, First Secretary, FCO, 1966-1975

Flanigan, Peter M, Assistant to the US President, 1970-74

Fogarty, Christopher W, Deputy Secretary, Treasury, 1972-76

Ford, Gerald R, US Vice-President, 1973-74; President, 1974-77

Forrester, Mark F, PS to the Prime Minister, 1971-75

Frank, Paul, State-Secretary, Federal German Foreign Ministry, 1970-74

Fretwell, Major John E, Counsellor (Commercial), British Embassy, Warsaw, 1971-73; Head of TRED, May-August, 1973; Head of EID (I), 1973-76

Freyche, Michel, Technical Counsellor in the General Secretariat of the French President, 1973-74

Friedmann, Jacques H, Chief Executive Secretary to the French Prime Minister, 1972-74

Frydenlund, Knut, Norwegian Foreign Minister, 1973-81

Fulbright, James W, US Senator (Democrat, Arkansas), 1945-74; Chairman, Senate Foreign Relations Committee, 1959-74

Gaja, Roberto, Secretary-General, Italian Foreign Ministry, 1969-75

Gallagher, F G Kenna, UK Permanent Representative to the OECD, Paris, 1971-77

Galley, Robert, French Minister of Transport, 1972-73; Minister of the Armed Forces, 1973-74

Galloway, William J, First Secretary and Counsellor, US Embassy, London, 1965-74

Gaulle, Charles de, French President, 1958-69

Ghorbal, Ashraf, Egyptian Ambassador, Washington, 1973-84

Giffard, C Sydney, Counsellor, Consul-General and Head of Chancery, British Embassy, Tel Aviv, 1972-75

Gildea, J R D, Assistant Secretary, DTI

Giscard d'Estaing, Valéry, French Minister of Finance and Economic Affairs, 1969-74

Goldschmidt, Bertrand, Director of International Relations, French Commissariat for Atomic Energy, 1970-77

Goldwater, Barry M, US Senator (Republican, Arizona), 1952-64 and 1969-87

Goodenough, Anthony M, PS to Baroness Tweedsmuir, 1972-74

Gordon Lennox, Lord Nicholas, Head of News Department, FCO, 1973-74; and NAD, 1974-75

Gore-Booth, David A, First Secretary, NENAD, 1971-74

Goulding, Marrack I, PS to Julian Amery, 1972-74

Grabert, Horst, State-Secretary and Chief of the Federal German Chancellor's Office, 1972-74

Graham, John A N, Counsellor and Head of Chancery, British Embassy, Washington, 1972-74

Grattan, Patrick H, APS to Secretary of State, 1971-74; First Secretary, FCO, 1974-76

Greenhill, Sir Denis, PUS, FCO, 1969-73

Greenwald, Joseph A, US Ambassador to the EC, Brussels, 1972-75

Gromyko, Andrei A, Soviet Foreign Minister, 1957-85

Guinness, John R S, First Secretary, FCO, seconded to CPRS, 1972-75

Haekkerup, Per, Danish Minister of Economic Affairs, 1971-73

Haferkamp, Wilhelm, Vice-President, EC Commission, 1973-84

Haig, Gen Alexander M, Chief of Staff to the US President, 1973-74

Haldeman, Harry Robbins (Bob), Chief of Staff to the US President, 1969-73

Hall, David J, Second (later First) Secretary, FCO, 1970-74

Hankey, Henry A A, AUS, FCO, 1969-74

Harding, Peter T, Assistant Secretary, DTI, 1973-74

Harris, Anthony D, First Secretary, FCO, 1972-75

Harris, L J, official, Cabinet Office

Hartke, Vance, US Senator (Democrat, Indiana), 1959-77

Hartman, Arthur A, Deputy Chief of Mission and Minister-Counsellor, US Mission to the EC, Brussels, 1972-74

Hartogh, A F K, Director-General for European Cooperation, Netherlands Ministry of Foreign Affairs

Hase, Karl-Günther von, Federal German Ambassador, London, 1970-77

Hatem (Hatim), Mohammed Abdul Kader, Egyptian Deputy Prime Minister, 1971-74

Hattersley, Roy S G, Minister of State, FCO, 1974-76

Hayman, Sir Peter, British High Commissioner, Ottawa, 1970-74

Healey, Denis W, Chancellor of the Exchequer, 1974-79

Heath, Edward R G, Prime Minister, 1970-74

Hedley-Miller, Mary E, Under-Secretary, Treasury, 1973-83

Henderson, Sir Nicholas, British Ambassador, Bonn, 1972-75

Heseltine, Michael, Minister for Aerospace and Shipping, DTI, 1972-74

Hibbert, Reginald, British Minister, Bonn, 1972-75

Hilal, Ahmed Izzedin, Egyptian Minister of Petroleum, 1973-84

Hill, Robert C, Assistant Secretary for ISA, US Department of Defense, 1973-74

Hillenbrand, Martin J, US Ambassador, Bonn, 1972-76

Hockaday, Arthur P, Under-Secretary, Cabinet Office, 1972-73; Deputy Under-Secretary of State, MoD, 1973-76

Howe, Sir Geoffrey, Minister of Trade and Consumer Affairs, DTI, 1972-74

Howell, David A R, Minister of State, Department of Energy, 1974

Humphrey, Hubert H, US Senator (Democrat, Minnesota), 1971-78

Hunt, Sir John, Second Permanent Secretary, Cabinet Office, 1972-73; Secretary of the Cabinet, 1973-79

Hunt, Rex M, First Secretary, FCO, 1972-74

Hussein ibn Talal, King of Jordan, 1952-99

Hyland, William G, NSC staff member, 1969-73; Director of Intelligence, US State Department, 1973-75

Ismail, General Mohamed Hafiz, adviser to the Egyptian President on National Security, 1971-74

Jackson, Henry M, US Senator (Democrat, Washington), 1953-83

Jackson, John E, Head of Defence Department, FCO, 1973-75

James, Alan G, First Secretary (later Counsellor), US Embassy, London, 1968-75

James, Cynlais M, Head of WED, 1971-75

Jamieson, Kenneth D, Minister, UKMIS, New York, 1970-74

Jarring, Gunnar, UN Secretary-General's Special Envoy on the Middle Eastern situation, 1967-90

Javits, Jacob K, US Senator (Republican, New York), 1957-80

Jellicoe, Earl, Lord Privy Seal, 1970-73

Jobert, Michel, French Foreign Minister, 1973-74

Jørgensen, Anke, Danish Prime Minister, 1972-73

Joseph, Sir Keith, Secretary of State for Social Services, 1970-74

Katz, Julius L, Deputy Assistant Secretary of State for International Resources and Food Policy, US State Department, 1968-74

Kaufman, Robert E, Energy Attaché (from 1975 First Secretary), US Embassy, London, 1972-77

Keating, Justin, Republic of Ireland Minister for Industry and Commerce, 1973-77

Kedah, Zvi, Minister, Israeli Embassy, London, 1973-77

Kennedy, David M, US Permanent Representative to NATO, 1972-73

Kennedy, Edward M, US Senator (Democrat, Massachusetts), 1962-

Kershaw, J Anthony, Parliamentary Under-Secretary of State, FCO, 1970-73

Khammash, Gen Amer Baseem, Chief of Staff of the Jordan Arab Army

Killick, Sir John, British Ambassador, Moscow, 1971-73; DUS, FCO, 1973-75

Kirk, Peter M, MP (Conservative, Saffron Walden), 1965-77; Leader of the Conservative Delegation to the European Parliament, 1973-77

Kissinger, Henry A, Special Assistant to the US President for National Security Affairs, 1969-75; US Secretary of State, 1973-77

Kosygin, Alexei N, Soviet Premier, 1964-80

Krapf, Franz, Federal German Permanent Representative to NATO, 1971-76

Kuznetsov, Vasiliy V, Soviet First Deputy Foreign Minister, 1955-77

Laird, Melvin R, US Secretary of Defense, 1969-73; Counsellor to the US President for Domestic Affairs, 1973-74

Lardinois, Petrus Josephus, EC Agricultural Commissioner, 1973-76

Lavalette, Alain Lucien Louis Lacroix de, Head of Special Services, EEC, 1973-84

Lavelle, Roger G, Assistant Secretary, Treasury, 1968-75

Le Bailly, Vice-Adm Sir Louis, Director-General of Intelligence, MoD, 1972-75

Lebsanft, Ulrich, Federal German Permanent Representative to the EC

Ledwidge, W Bernard J, British Ambassador, Tel Aviv, 1972-75

Lee, H S, Assistant Secretary, Treasury

Lennep, Jonkheer Emile van, Secretary-General, OECD, Paris, 1969-84

Le Quesne, Charles (from 1974 Sir) Martin, DUS, FCO, 1971-74

Levy, Walter J, international oil consultant; Consultant to the US State Department, Office of Under-Secretary and Assistant Secretaries, 1960-80

Ligon, Duke, Director, Office of Oil and Gas, US Department of the Interior, 1973-74

Liverman, John Gordon, Deputy Secretary, DTI, 1972-74

Livingston, Robert Gerald, NSC staff member, 1972-73

Lloyd Jones, Richard A, Assistant Secretary, MoD, 1970-74

Lobdell, Brig Gen Harrison, Director, European Division, Office of the US Assistant Secretary of Defense (ISA), 1971-74

Lockton, Guy Patrick, Second Secretary, FCO, 1971-75

Long, Russell B, US Senator (Democrat, Louisiana), 1948-86; Chairman, Senate Finance Committee, 1966-81

Louis, Victor, Moscow correspondent of *The Evening News*

Love, John A, Governor of Colorado, 1963-73; Head of the US Energy Policy Office, June-December 1973

Lunkov, Nikolai M, Soviet Ambassador, London, 1973-80

Luns, Joseph M A H, NATO Secretary-General, 1971-83

Lynden, Baron Diederic Wolter van, Director-General for Political Affairs, Netherlands Foreign Ministry, 1970-74

McCaffrey, Thomas D, Head of News Department, FCO, 1974-76

McCloskey, Robert J, US Deputy Assistant Secretary of State, Special Assistant for Press Relations, 1968-73; US Ambassador, Nicosia, 1973-74

McFadzean, Francis S (Frank), Managing Director of Royal Dutch Shell Group of Companies, 1964-76

MacInnes, Keith G, First Secretary, FCO, 1970-74

McIntyre, Sir Laurence, Australian Permanent Representative to the UN, 1970-75

McLaren, Robin J T, Deputy Head of WOD, 1974-75

MacLennan, David R, First Secretary, FCO, 1972-75

Macmillan, Maurice, Secretary of State for Employment, 1972-73; Paymaster General, 1973-74

McNally, Tom, Political Adviser to Foreign and Commonwealth Secretary, 1974-76

McNamara, Robert S, US Secretary of Defense, 1961-68; President of International Bank for Reconstruction and Development, 1968-81

Maitland, Donald J D, on secondment to Prime Minister's Office, 1970-73; UK Permanent Representative to the UN, New York, 1973-74

Malagodi, Giovanni Francesco, Italian Treasury Minister, 1972-73

Malmgren, Harald B (Hal), US Deputy Trade Representative, 1972-74

Mansfield, Michael J, US Senator (Democrat, Montana), 1952-76; Senate Leader, 1961-76

Margerie, Emmanuel Jacquin de, Director of European Department, French Foreign Ministry, 1972-74

Marnham, John E, British Ambassador, Tunis, 1973-76

Marshall, Charles J, Canadian Deputy Permanent Representative to NATO, 1971-74

Marshall, Peter H R, Head of Financial Policy and Aid Department, 1971-73; AUS, FCO, 1973-75

Marshall, Sir Robert, Secretary (Industry), DTI, 1970-73; Second Permanent Secretary, Department of Education, 1973-78

Mason, Sir Frederick, UK Permanent Representative to the Office of the UN and other International Organisations, Geneva, 1971-73

Masoud, Muhammad Ibrahim, Saudi Arabian Deputy Foreign Minister

Medici, Giuseppe, Italian Foreign Minister, 1972-73

Meir, Golda, Israeli Prime Minister, 1969-74

Menzies, Arthur R, Canadian Permanent Representative to NATO, 1972-76

Messmer, Pierre A J, French Prime Minister, 1972-74

Meulen, Jozeph B M van der, Belgian Permanent Representative to the EC, 1959-79

Mills, Wilbur D, US Congressman (Democrat, Arkansas), 1939-77; Chairman of House Ways and Means Committee, 1958-74

Mitchell, Derek Jack, Second Permanent Secretary, Treasury, 1973-77

Moberly, John C, Counsellor, British Embassy, Washington, 1969-75

Mohammed Reza Pahlavi, Shah of Iran, 1941-79

Monnet, Jean, Chairman of the Action Committee for a United States of Europe, 1956-75

Moro, Aldo, Italian Foreign Minister, 1973-74

Moss, David J, First Secretary, FCO, 1970-74

Mountfield, P, Assistant Secretary, Treasury

Moussadeq, Mohhamed, Iranian Prime Minister, 1951-53

Muhiuddin, Zakaria, Egyptian Prime Minister, 1965-66

Muir, Richard J S, Second Secretary, FCO, 1973-74

Mumford, William F, Assistant Secretary, MoD, 1967-73; PPS to the Defence Secretary, 1973-74

Muskie, Edmund S, US Senator (Democrat, Maine), 1959-80

Myerson, Jacob M, Deputy Chief and Minister Counsellor, US Mission to the EC, Brussels, 1970-75

Nairne Patrick D, DUS, MoD, 1970-73; Second Permanent Secretary, Cabinet Office, 1973-75

Nakasone, Yasuhiro, Japanese Minister of International Trade and Industry, 1972-74

Nanteuil, Luc de la Barre de, Director for Economic Affairs, French Foreign Ministry, 1970-76

Nash, Kenneth T, AUS (Defence Staff), MoD, 1972-74

Nasser, Gamal Abdel, Egyptian President, 1956-70

Nazer (Nazir), Hisham, President, Saudi Arabian Central Organisation for Planning

Neale, Sir Alan, Permanent Secretary, MAFF, 1973-78

Neguib (Nagib), Gen Mohamed, Egyptian President, 1953-54

Nelissen, Roelof J, Netherlands Minister of Finance, 1971-73

Nixon, Richard M, US President, 1969-74

Norbury, Brian M, PS to the Secretary of the Cabinet, 1970-73; Assistant Secretary, MoD, 1973-79

Norgaard, Ivar, Danish Minister for Foreign Economic Affairs and Nordic Relations, 1971-73

O'Brien, Leslie Kenneth, Governor of the Bank of England, 1966-73

Oldenburg, Troels V A, Assistant Under-Secretary for Political Affairs, Danish Foreign Ministry, 1968-74

O'Neill, Robert James, Assistant Secretary, Cabinet office, 1972-75

Ortoli, Francois-Xavier, President of the EC Commission, 1973-76

Overton, Hugh T A, Head of NAD, 1971-74

Owen, John Glendwr, Under-Secretary, Treasury, 1959-73

Pakenham, Michael A, PS to the Chancellor of the Duchy of Lancaster, 1971; on secondment to the Cabinet Office, 1972; First Secretary, FCO, 1972-74.

Palliser, Sir Michael, UK Permanent Representative to the EC, Brussels, 1973-75

Parsons, Anthony D, AUS, FCO, 1971-74; British Ambassador, Tehran, 1974-79

Part, Sir Antony, Permanent Secretary, DTI, 1970-74

Pastinen, Ilkka, Assistant to the UN Secretary-General, 1971-75

Peck, Sir Edward, UK Permanent Representative to NATO, 1970-75

Peres, Shimon, Israeli Minister of Transport and Communications, 1970-74

Peterson, Colin Vyvyan, PS (Appointments) to the Prime Minister, Treasury, 1973-74

Peterson, Peter G, Assistant to the US President for International Economic Affairs, 1971-72; US Secretary of Commerce, 1972-73

Phelps, Anthony J, Under-Secretary, Treasury, 1968-73

Piketty, Gérard, Technical Counsellor for Energy and Atomic Questions, French Ministry of Industrial and Scientific Development, 1969-74

Pocock, Carmichael C P (Michael), Managing Director, Royal Dutch Shell Group of Companies, 1970-79

Pompidou, Georges, French President, 1969-74

Powell, Charles D, First Secretary and PS to the British Ambassador, Washington, 1971-74

Prior, James, Lord President of the Council and Leader of the House of Commons, 1972-74

Puaux, François, Political Director, French Foreign Ministry, 1972-75

Qadhafi (Qaddafi/Gaddafi), Col Mu'ammar Muhammad al-, Chairman of Libya's Revolutionary Command Council, 1969-77

Raeymaekers, Jacques, Belgian diplomat

Rampton, Sir Jack, Second Permanent Secretary and Secretary (Industrial Development), DTI, 1972-74; PUS, Department of Energy, 1974-80

Ramsbotham, Sir Peter, British Ambassador, Tehran, 1971-74, and Washington, 1974-77

Rawlinson, Sir Peter, Attorney General, 1970-74

Ray, Dixie Lee, Chairman of US Atomic Energy Commission, 1973-75

Reeve, Anthony, First Secretary, FCO, 1970-73, and British Embassy, Washington, 1973-78

Renwick, Robin W, First Secretary, British Embassy, Paris, 1972-76

Reston, James (Scotty), Vice-President, *New York Times*, 1969-74

Reuter, Col, Chief of Foreign Liaison, IDF

Richardson, Elliot Lee, US Secretary of Defense, 1972-73; Attorney-General, May-October 1973

Richardson, Gordon, Governor of the Bank of England, 1973-83

Rippon, Geoffrey, Secretary of State for the Environment, 1972-74

Roberts, J, Under-Secretary, Cabinet Office

Robinson, John A, AUS, FCO, 1971-74

Rodman, Peter W, NSC staff member, 1969-77; Special Assistant to Henry Kissinger, 1972-77

Rogers, William P, US Secretary of State, 1969-1973

Rogerson, Major, UN military observer, Syria

Roper, John C A, British Ambassador, Luxembourg, 1970-75

Rose, Clive M, AUS, FCO, 1971-73; Head of UK Delegation to the MBFR talks, Vienna, 1973-76

Rose, François Tricornot de, French Permanent Representative to NATO, 1970-75

Rosenthal, Benjamin S, US Congressman (Democrat, New York), 1963-83

Rostow, Walt Whitman, Professor of Economics and History, University of Texas

Rothnie, Alan K, British Ambassador, Jedda, 1972-76

Rothschild Lord, Director General and First Permanent Under-Secretary, CPRS, Cabinet Office, 1971-74

Rouillon, Fernand, Assistant Director, Middle Eastern Department, French Foreign Ministry, 1970-75

Royle, Anthony, Parliamentary Under-Secretary of State, FCO, 1970-74

Rumsfeld, Donald H, US Permanent Representative to NATO, 1973-74

Rush, Kenneth, US Deputy Secretary of Defense, 1972-73; Deputy Secretary of State, 1973-74; Acting Secretary of State September 1973

Rusk, Dean, US Secretary of State, 1961-69

Sa'ad al-Abdullah, Sheikh, Kuwaiti Defence Minister

Sabah, Sheikh Sabah al-Ahmad al-Jaber al-, Kuwaiti Foreign Minister, 1963-78

Sabri, Ali, Egyptian Vice-President, 1970-71

Sadat, Anwar al-, Egyptian President, 1970-81

Sadiq, General Muhammad, Egyptian Defence Minister, 1971-73

Saqqaf, Sheikh Omar, Saudi Arabian Minister of State for Foreign Affairs

Sassen, Emmanuel M J A, Netherlands Permanent Representative to the EC

Saunders, Harold (Hal), NSC staff member, 1961-74

Scali, John A, Special Consultant for foreign affairs to the US President, 1971-73; US Permanent Representative to the UN, New York, 1973-75

Scheel, Walter, Federal German Vice-Chancellor and Foreign Minister, 1969-74

Schlesinger, James R, US Secretary of Defense, 1973-75

Schmelzer, W K Norbert, Netherlands Foreign Minister, 1971-73

Schmidt, Helmut H W, Federal German Minister of Finance, 1972-74

Schumann, Maurice, French Foreign Minister, 1969-73

Scowcroft, Lieut-Gen Brent, Military Assistant to US President, 1972-73; US Deputy Assistant to the President for National Security Affairs, 1973-75

Shultz, George P, US Secretary of the Treasury, 1972-74

Simon, William E, Head of US Federal Energy Office, 1973-74

Simonet, Henri F, Vice-President, EC Commission, 1973-77

Simpson, Oliver, Under-Secretary, Cabinet Office, 1969-74

Sisco, Joseph J, US Assistant Secretary of State, Middle East-South Asia, 1969-74; Under-Secretary of State for Political Affairs, 1974-76

Smith, Edward J, Under-Secretary, MAFF, 1971-74

Smith, Howard F T, Deputy Secretary, Cabinet Office, 1972-75

Smith, Jackson, US Deputy Permanent Representative to NATO

Smith, Thomas W M, First Secretary, US Embassy, London, 1972-75

Soames, Sir Christopher, British Ambassador, Paris, 1968-72; Vice President of the EC Commission and Commissioner for External Affairs, 1973-77

Sohm, Earl D, Minister, US Embassy, London, 1972-74

Sonnenfeldt, Helmut, Senior NSC Staff member for Europe and East-West Relations, 1969-74

Souviron, Jean-Pierre, Deputy Director of the Cabinet of the French Foreign Minister, 1973-74

Spain, Stephen W, Under-Secretary and Head of Oil Policy Division, DTI, 1973-74

Spencer, Rosemary J, First Secretary, UKDEL Brussels, 1972-74

Spierenburg, Dirk P, Netherlands Permanent Representative to NATO, 1970-73

Spinks, C K, Assistant Secretary, Department of the Environment

Spreckley, John N T, First Secretary, British Embassy, Paris, 1970-75

Staden, Berndt von, Federal German Ambassador, Washington, 1973-79

Staerck, André Marie de, Belgian Permanent Representative to NATO, 1952-76

Stark, Andrew A S, British Ambassador, Copenhagen, 1971-76

Steel, David E C, Deputy Chairman, BP, 1972-75

Sterner, Michael Edmund, Country Director for Egyptian Affairs, US State Department, 1971-74

Stoel, Max van der, Netherlands Foreign Minister, 1973-77

Stoessel, Walter J, US Assistant Secretary of State for European Affairs, 1972-74

Sullivan, William H, US Deputy Assistant Secretary of State for East Asia, 1969-73; US Ambassador, Manila, 1973-77

Sutcliffe, J W R, BP representative

Svart, Anker, Danish Permanent Representative to NATO, 1973-81

Sykes, Richard A, Minister, British Embassy Washington, 1972-75

Tanaka, Kaknei, Japanese Prime Minister, 1972-74

Tarrant, J, FSO, US State Department

Taylor, John L, Head of ISED, 1972-73; AUS, FCO, 1973-75

Tekoah, Yosef, Israeli Permanent Representative to the UN, New York, 1968-75

Thomson, George M, EC Commissioner with special responsibility for Regional Policy, 1973-77

Thomson, John A, Minister and Deputy Permanent Representative, UKDEL, NATO, 1972-73; AUS, FCO, 1973-76

Thorn, Gaston, Luxembourg Foreign Minister, 1969-80

Thorning-Petersen, Rudolph, Danish diplomat

Tickell, Crispin C C, Head of WOD, 1972-75

Tomkins, Sir Edward, British Ambassador, Paris, 1972-75

Trend, Sir Burke, Secretary to the Cabinet, 1963-73

Tripp, John P, British Ambassador, Tripoli, 1970-74

Tweedsmuir of Belhelvie, Baroness, Minister of State, FCO, 1972-75

Urwick, Alan B, Counsellor, British Embassy, Cairo, 1971-73; Assistant Secretary, CPRS, 1973-75

Vaillaud, Michel L, Head of French Oil and Gas Directorate, 1969-73

Vanick, Charles, US Congressman (Democrat, Ohio), 1954-81

Vest, George S, Special Assistant to US Secretary of State for Press Relations, 1973-74

Vishinsky, Andrei Y, Soviet Foreign Minister, 1949-53

Volcker, Paul A, Deputy Under-Secretary for Monetary Affairs, US Treasury Department, 1969-74

Waldheim, Kurt, UN Secretary-General, 1972-82

Walker, Harold B, First Secretary (Commercial), British Embassy, Washington, 1970-73; Counsellor, British Embassy, Jedda, 1973-76

Walker, Peter E, Secretary of State for Trade and Industry, 1972-74

Watson, Sir (Noel) Duncan, DUS, FCO, 1972-75

Watts, A R M, Assistant Secretary, DTI

Webster, B M, PPS to the Chancellor of the Duchy of Lancaster

Weir, Michael S, Counsellor and Head of Chancery, UKMIS, New York, 1971-74; AUS, FCO, 1974-77

Well, Günther W van, Political Director, Federal German Foreign Ministry, 1972-77

Wellenstein, Edmund P, Director-General for External Relations, EC Commission, 1973-76

Werner, Pierre, Luxembourg Prime Minister and Minister of Finance, 1969-74

Weston, Michael C S, First Secretary, UKMIS, New York, 1970-74

Whitehead, George S, AUS, FCO, 1972-75

Whitelaw, William, Secretary of State for Northern Ireland, 1972-73; for Employment, 1973-74

Wickham, Maj Gen John A, Military Assistant to US Secretary of Defense, 1973-76

Wiggin, Charles D, AUS, FCO, 1971-74

Wilford, Kenneth M, AUS, FCO, 1969-73; DUS, FCO, 1973-75

Williams, Leonard, Deputy Secretary (Energy), DTI, 1973-74; Department of Energy, 1974-76

Willumsen, Kjeld E, Minister, Danish Embassy, London, 1972-76

Wilson, J Harold, Prime Minister, 1974-76

Wilton, Arthur J, British Ambassador, Kuwait, 1970-74

Woessner, William M, First Secretary (later Counsellor), US Embassy London, 1972-77

Wright, J Oliver, DUS, FCO, 1972-75

Wright, Patrick R H, Head of MED, 1972-74

Wright, Paul H G, British Ambassador, Beirut, 1971-75

Wurth, Pierre, Secretary-General, Luxembourg Foreign Ministry, 1971-77

Yamani, Sheikh Ahmed Zaki, Saudi Arabian Minister of Petroleum and Mineral Resources, 1962-86; Chairman, OAPEC, 1974-75

Youde, Edward, AUS, FCO, 1973-74

Zayyat, Mohamed Hassan el-, Egyptian Foreign Minister, 1972-73; Adviser to the Egyptian President, 1973-75

Ziegler, Ronald Lewis, Press Secretary to President Nixon, 1969-74

DOCUMENT SUMMARIES

24 October 1972 – 27 April 1973

	DOCUMENT	DATE	MAIN SUBJECT
1	Letter: Heath to Nixon Douglas-Home papers	**1972** 24 Oct	Summarises results of the EC Summit in Paris.
2	Washington diplomatic report 480/72 AMU 2/3	15 Nov	Analyses US foreign policy following Nixon's re-election.
3	Letter: Carrington to Heath AMU 3/507/1	29 Nov	Expresses concern over deterioration of confidence in US/European relations.
4	Letter: R T Armstrong to Acland MWE 3/304/2	12 Dec	Advises on desirability of speaking 'from a single [EC] position' in Washington.
5	Letter: Rothschild to R Marshall SMG 2/1	12 Dec	Reports W Levy's proposals for an alliance of oil consumers.
6	Minute: Chalmers to Whitehead SMG 2/1	14 Dec	Criticises Levy's proposals.
7	Letter: Overton to Graham AMU 3/507/1	15 Dec	Forecasts a 'busy and difficult year for US/Europe relations'.
8	Letter: Acland to R T Armstrong CAB 164/1232	19 Dec	Responds to Armstrong's suggestions for EC/US dialogue.
9	Letter: Graham to Overton AMU 3/507/1	28 Dec	Considers Britain's role in transatlantic relations.
10	Minute: Robinson to J O Wright MWE 3/304/2	**1973** 1 Jan	Considers response to the US Administration's 'Europe Year'.
11	Letter: Acland to Bridges MWE 3/304/1	16 Jan	Records conversation between Douglas-Home, Scheel and Schumann.
12	Brussels tel 25 MWE 3/304/1	17 Jan	Reports meeting of Political Directors of the EC Nine: transatlantic relations and Nixon's projected European visit.
13	Minute: Greenhill to Acland SMG 2/1	18 Jan	Assesses need for urgency in tackling the oil problem.

14	Letter: Cromer to Greenhill AMU 3/507/1	19 Jan	Examines state of transatlantic relations, with annex on the 'interrelationship of issues'.
15	Minute: Brimelow to Greenhill Brimelow papers	22 Jan	Covers draft brief on 'Operation Hullabaloo'.
16	Record of meeting of the Oil Policy Committee NB 12/1	24 Jan	Considers briefing of Heath on oil policy.
17	Minute: Brimelow to Greenhill Brimelow papers	25 Jan	Objects to Soviet draft agreement on non-use of nuclear weapons.
18	Extract from steering brief AMU 3/548/3	25 Jan	Advises on Heath's forthcoming Washington talks with Nixon.
19	Record of discussion: Heath/Nixon AMU 3/548/8	1 Feb	US/European commercial and monetary relations.
20	Record of discussion: Heath/Nixon AMU 3/548/8	2 Feb	East-West relations.
21	Record of discussion: Heath/Nixon AMU 3/548/8	2 Feb	Energy policy.
22	Record of discussion: Heath/Nixon AMU 3/548/8	2 Feb	'Operation Hullabaloo'.
23	Memo by P E Walker ES(73) 7 CAB 134/3606	8 Feb	Covers report on oil policy for Cabinet Ministerial Committee on Economic Strategy.
24	Letter: Dunnett to Trend AMU 3/507/1	9 Feb	Proposes establishment of an inter-departmental committee to review transatlantic relations.
25	Minute: Overton to Hankey AMU 3/548/8	13 Feb	Offers personal impressions of Heath's Washington visit.
26	Washington tel 678 MWE 3/304/1	16 Feb	Reports on Soames's visit to Washington and discussions on EC/US relations.
27	Record of conversation: Heath/Hafiz Ismail NFW 3/322/1	20 Feb	The Middle East 'was approaching a difficult and dangerous stage'.

28	Memo by P E Walker ES(73) 8 CAB 134/3607	21 Feb	Oil policy: consumer-government cooperation.
29	Washington diplomatic report 180/73 AMU 3/548/3	22 Feb	Comments on Heath's Washington visit.
30	Letter: Peck to Greenhill MWE 3/304/1	22 Feb	Considers US's relations with NATO allies.
31	Record of conversation: Douglas-Home/P G Peterson MWE 3/304/4	22 Feb	US/European economic and military relations.
32	Minute: Brimelow to Greenhill Brimelow papers	23 Feb	Reports on progress with 'Hullabaloo', and its potential for diplomatic embarrassment.
33	Letter: Trend to Dunnett AMU 3/507/1	1 Mar	Recommends monthly PUS meetings on US/UK relations.
34	Letter: Archer to H B Walker AMU 1/2	1 Mar	Enquires about origins of the expression 'Year of Europe'.
35	Washington tel 819 Douglas-Home papers	1 Mar	Reports Kissinger's request for HMG's comments on No. 36.
36	Washington tel 820 Douglas-Home papers	1 Mar	Transmits memo describing Hafiz Ismail's views on Middle Eastern peace settlement.
37	Minutes of Cabinet meeting PREM 15/1459	3 Mar	Records discussion of currency crisis and prospects for a joint EC currency float.
38	Washington tel 851 Douglas-Home papers	3 Mar	Message from Nixon to Heath complaining about UK/German approach to currency crisis.
39	Tel 586 to Washington Douglas-Home papers	4 Mar	Message from Heath assuring Nixon that European integration should serve interests of Atlantic alliance.
40	Tel 587 to Washington Douglas-Home papers	4 Mar	Comments on No. 36.
41	DTI memo: EUM(73) 15 CAB 134/3611	5 Mar	Examines EC enlargement and the GATT negotiations.
42	UKREP Brussels tel 1173 MWE 3/304/1	5 Mar	Records EC Council meeting: Soames reports on visit to US and transatlantic relations.

43	Tel 195 to Bonn Douglas-Home papers	6 Mar	Message from Heath to Brandt on European solution to currency crisis.
44	Letter: Cromer to Brimelow Brimelow papers	7 Mar	Covers record of Brimelow's conversation with Kissinger in Washington: 'Hullabaloo' and the transatlantic relationship.
45	Bonn tel 331 Douglas-Home papers	8 Mar	Transmits message from Brandt to Heath: currency crisis and prospects for joint EC float.
46	Tel 201 to Bonn Douglas-Home papers	10 Mar	Transmits message to Brandt regarding joint float.
47	Bonn tel 338 Douglas-Home papers	11 Mar	Transmits message from Brandt to Heath: rejects British proposal for 'unlimited and unconditional credit'.
48	UKREP Brussels tel 1320 PREM 15/1459	11 Mar	Reports on European Council meeting: UK unable to join common float on the basis of EC Commission proposals.
49	UKREP Brussels tel 1322 PREM 15/1459	12 Mar	EC Council statement on the monetary crisis.
50	Minute: Heath to Barber PREM 15/1459	12 Mar	Expresses disappointment at UK's inability to participate in EC currency float.
51	Letter: B L Crowe to Archer AMU 1/2	12 Mar	Explains origins of the 'Year of Europe'.
52	Tel 218 to Bonn Douglas-Home papers	15 Mar	Transmits message from Heath to Brandt on latest EC monetary arrangements.
53	UKREP Brussels tel 1512 PREM 15/1460	20 Mar	Reports that Pompidou stressed that until EC was back on the road to economic and monetary union, 'Europe was blocked'.
54	UKREP Brussels tel 1513 PREM 15/1460	20 Mar	Assesses French reactions to continued floating of pound sterling.
55	Cairo despt 2/4 NFW 3/322/1	20 Mar	Predicts that the most likely result of an unbroken Arab-Israeli deadlock was 'a radicalisation of the conflict on the Arab side'.
56	Tel 735 to Washington AMU 3/548/7	22 Mar	Informs about Shultz's London visit and discussions on US trade

			policy.
57	Minute: Gore-Booth to Parsons NFW 3/548/2	29 Mar	Considers British policy towards the Arab-Israeli dispute.
58	CPRS memo for the Cabinet Ministerial Committee on Europe SMG 12/598/1	3 Apr	Covers paper by Boardman on UK objectives in an EC energy policy.
59	Washington tel 1223 Brimelow papers	5 Apr	Informs Brimelow on 'Hullabaloo'.
60	Washington tel 1224 Brimelow papers	5 Apr	Conveys memo by Kissinger on 'Hullabaloo'.
61	Washington tel 1225 Brimelow papers	5 Apr	Transmits latest American draft of US/Soviet agreement.
62	Minute: J J B Hunt to Heath CAB 164/1232	5 Apr	Informs that Ministers had agreed 'with some reservation' to favourable response to Kissinger's request for a concepts paper.
63	Letter: Parsons to Adams NFW 3/322/1	10 Apr	Expresses frustration over deadlock in the Arab-Israeli dispute.
64	Extract from minutes of the Cabinet Ministerial Committee on Economic Strategy, ES(73) 3rd mtg CAB 134/3606	11 Apr	Endorses recommendations in No. 23.
65	Note by Trend, Hunt and H F T Smith CAB 130/671	12 Apr	Note covering summary of paper, 'The next ten years in East-West and transatlantic relations', and accompanying speaking notes.
66	Washington despt 2/15/1 NFW 3/304/1	17 Apr	Analyses US policy in the Middle East.
67	Letter: Greenhill to Cromer AMU 3/507/1	17 Apr	Reports monthly meetings of PUSs on transatlantic relations.
68	Letter: Cromer to Greenhill MWE 6/304/1	19 Apr	Describes US Trade Reform Bill.
69	Record of meeting: Trend/Kissinger CAB 164/1233	19 Apr	Discussion of US/European relations.
70	Washington tel 1361 AMU 3/507/1	23 Apr	Transmits text of Kissinger's speech to Associated Press annual

luncheon: '1973 is the Year of Europe'.

71	Washington tel 1362 AMU 3/507/1	23 Apr	Reports request that HMG 'should say something to welcome' Kissinger's speech.
72	Washington tel 1370 AMU 3/507/1	23 Apr	Comments on the significance of Kissinger's speech.
73	Letter: Trend to Greenhill SMG 25/304/1	24 Apr	Reports that Washington meeting had been a 'dress rehearsal' for Kissinger's speech.
74	Minute: Trend to Heath CAB 164/1233	24 Apr	Covers personal account of meeting with Kissinger on 19 April.
75	Paris tel 588 AMU 3/507/1	26 Apr	Reports official French reactions to Kissinger's speech.
76	Minute: Greenhill to Acland SMG 12/598/4	26 Apr	Considers EC policies towards Middle Eastern oil producers.
77	Minute by Overton AMU 3/507/1	27 Apr	Summarises FCO's position on Kissinger's speech.
78	Tel 972 to Washington MWE 3/304/1	27 Apr	Reports on EC Political Directors' discussion of US/European relations.
79	Extract from speech by Douglas-Home CAB 164/1233	27 Apr	Endorses Kissinger's address as 'realistic and timely'.

27 April – 30 July 1973

80	Letter: Parsons to Moberly NFW 3/548/2	27 Apr	Assesses UNSC's handling of the Arab-Israeli dispute.
81	Minute: Trend to Heath Douglas-Home papers	2 May	Advises on UK response to Kissinger's initiative.
82	Cairo tel 404 NFW 3/322/1	2 May	Reports Sadat's speech on the Arab-Israeli conflict.
83	Cairo tel 405 NFW 3/322/1	2 May	Considers significance of Sadat's speech.
84	Letter: Bridges to Norbury CAB 164/1233	3 May	Endorses views expressed in No. 81.
85	Minute: Tickell to Wiggin MWE 3/304/1	4 May	Expresses doubts about value of a new 'Atlantic Charter'.

86	Minute: Robinson to J O Wright MWE 3/304/1	7 May	Covers submissions by M D Butler on handling of EC/US relations.
87	Letter: Cromer to Brimelow AMU 3/507/1	8 May	Considers reactions to Kissinger's speech.
88	Minute: Overton to Wiggin AMU 3/507/1	9 May	Covers notes on Kissinger's initiative and Nixon's political position.
89	Record of conversation: Douglas-Home/Kissinger AMU 3/548/14	10 May	Discussion of the Middle East, US/European relations, and energy.
90	UKDEL NATO tel 8 Saving MWE 3/304/1	11 May	Reports informal NAC meeting to discuss Kissinger's speech.
91	Washington tel 1545 NFW 2/4	11 May	Reports discussion with Sisco of forthcoming UNSC meeting on the Arab-Israeli dispute.
92	Tel 1071 to Washington NFW 2/4	14 May	Comments on No. 91: FCO disagrees with US approach.
93	Washington tel 1565 NFW 2/4	14 May	Informs of further discussion with Sisco, who remained sceptical about outcome of UNSC debate.
94	Tel 328 to Bonn NFW 2/17	16 May	Parsons comments on current state of play in the Middle East.
95	Brief for Heath Brimelow papers	16 May	Updates on 'Hullabaloo': covers latest draft of Agreement on the Prevention of Nuclear War.
96	Paris tel 691 PREM 15/1554	18 May	Informs Greenhill of Kissinger's talks with Jobert on US/European relations.
97	Exchange of minutes: Overton/Wiggin AMU 3/507/1	21 & 29 May	Examines significance of Kissinger's emphasis on 'linkage' between trade, money and defence.
98	Extract from record of conversation: Heath/Pompidou PREM 15/1555	22 May	Talks on transatlantic relations and Nixon's forthcoming visit to Europe.
99	Letter: Moberly to Parsons NFW 3/304/1	22 May	Reports little prospect of a US move in the Arab-Israeli dispute.
100	Tel 162 to Tel Aviv NFW 3/408/1	22 May	Informs of conversation with Abba Eban: 'no good could come

of Security Council debate'.

101	Extract from minute of Cabinet European Unit, EUU(73) 12th mtg CAB 134/3625	23 May	Impressions of Heath's meeting with Pompidou.
102	UKREP Brussels tel 2780 MWE 3/304/1	25 May	Reports 'unsatisfactory working dinner' of Political Directors: EC/US relations.
103	Paris tel 728 MWE 3/304/1	26 May	Speculates on French position regarding EC/US relations.
104	UKREP Brussels tel 275 MWE 3/304/1	26 May	Reports that French were 'entirely isolated' at Political Directors' meeting.
105	Tel 1149 to Washington PREM 15/1554	29 May	Message from Heath to Nixon on Pompidou and EC/US relations.
106	Tel 400 to UKMIS New York NFW 3/22/1	31 May	Informs of conversation with El-Zayyat on Egypt's policy towards Israel.
107	Tel 52 Luxembourg MWE 3/304/1	4 June	Summarises US account of Nixon/Pompidou meeting (30 May-1 June).
108	Record of meeting: Trend/Kissinger CAB 164/1233	4 June	Discussion of the future of Kissinger's 'Year of Europe' initiative.
109	Minute: Heath to Douglas-Home NFW 3/548/2	4 June	Expresses concern at Eban's failure to understand dangers facing Israel.
110	Tel 450 to Paris MWE 3/304/1	6 June	Reports ministerial EPC meeting: response to US initiative.
111	Minute: Parsons to Acland NFW 3/548/2	7 June	Examines Western interests in the Middle East.
112	Minute: Douglas-Home to Heath NFW 3/548/2	7 June	Argues the need to persuade the US to put pressure on the Israelis.
113	Minute: J O Wright to Greenhill MWE 3/304/1	7 June	Covers note on transatlantic relations and US 'grievances'.
114	Paris tel 782 CAB 164/1233	7 June	Reports French impressions of EPC meeting.
115	Letter: Trend to Cromer CAB 164/1233	8 June	Comments on Kissinger's likely disappointment with Jobert.

116	Tel 1234 Washington AMU 3/507/1	8 June	Greenhill asks to what extent Kissinger's warnings were to be taken seriously by Europeans?
117	Washington tel 1816 CAB 164/1233	10 June	Transmits message from Kissinger to Trend reporting Kissinger/Jobert meeting in Paris.
118	Record of meeting: Katz/J O Wright NB 2/2	11 June	Discussion of energy problems.
119	Washington tel 1821 Douglas-Home papers	11 June	Analyses US policy towards Europe.
120	Washington tel 1822 AMU 3/507/1	11 June	Answers Greenhill's questions in No. 116.
121	Minute: Acland to Parsons NFW 3/548/2	12 June	Transcribes Douglas-Home's manuscript note on No. 111.
122	Minute: Parsons to P R H Wright SMG 25/304/1	12 June	Reports Rogers's views on Arab use of oil as a 'political weapon'.
123	Washington tel 1859 CAB 164/1233	14 June	Reports receipt from White House of suggested headings for a Declaration of Principles.
124	Washington tel 1860 CAB 164/1233	14 June	Text of headings for Declaration of Principles.
125	Minute: Craig to Grattan NFW 2/4	15 June	Reports UNSC debate on the Arab-Israeli dispute.
126	Tel 1268 to Washington File destroyed	15 June	Requests Cromer to speak in support of Heath's forthcoming message to Nixon on the Middle East.
127	Tel 1269 to Washington PREM 15/1981	15 June	Transmits message from Heath urging Nixon to persuade Israelis to 'change their line' on negotiations.
128	Washington tel 1893 Brimelow papers	15 June	Reports that Sonnenfeldt hoped UK would 'make some welcoming noises' in NATO to announcement of US/Soviet nuclear agreement.
129	Minute: Tickell to Wiggin MWE 3/304/1	18 June	Reports on NATO ministerial meeting and argues that HMG should continue to occupy the middle ground on a transatlantic Declaration.

130	Minute: Douglas-Home to Heath MWE 3/304/1	18 June	Covers paper on US/European relations.
131	Tel 245 to UKDEL NATO Brimelow papers	18 June	Informs of forthcoming conclusion of US/Soviet agreement on the prevention of nuclear war.
132	Minute: Cable to Acland MWE 3/304/1	19 June	Covers brief for Heath on US/European relations.
133	Letter: R T Armstrong to Acland AMU 3/507/1	19 June	Reports Heath's criticisms of 'Year of Europe' initiative in conversation with Rostow.
134	Note by Trend for Cabinet Ministerial Committee on Economic Strategy, ES(OT)(73)1 CAB 165/989	19 June	Informs of the establishment and terms of reference of a Task Force on Oil Supplies.
135	Minute: Trend to Heath CAB 164/1234	19 June	Considers how to respond to Kissinger on EC/US relations.
136	Tel 247 to UKDEL NATO Brimelow papers	20 June	Instructs Peck on how to handle NATO response to US/Soviet agreement.
137	Cabinet minutes, GEN 161(73) 3rd mtg CAB 130/671	20 June	Discussion of future EC/US cooperation.
138	Minute: Parsons to Whitehead NB 12/3	21 June	Assesses threat to Middle Eastern oil supplies.
139	Letter: Moberly to Parsons NFW 3/304/1	21 June	Examines the US attitude towards the Arab-Israeli dispute.
140	UKDEL NATO tel 460 Brimelow papers	22 June	Reports NAC debate on the US/Soviet agreement on the prevention of nuclear war.
141	Washington tel 1322 AMU 18/1	25 June	Conveys message from Nixon to Heath on results of discussions with Brezhnev.
142	Letter: Cromer to Trend CAB 164/1234	25 June	Relates Kissinger's misplaced criticisms of Peck.
143	Record of meeting with oil company representatives SMG 1/2	27 June	Discussion of Middle Eastern situation and prospects for oil-consumer cooperation.
144	Minute: M D Butler to J O Wright	28 June	Assesses US/European relations.

MWE 3/304/1

145	Washington tel 2058 MWE 3/304/1	1 July	Reports Kissinger's account of talks with Jobert at San Clemente.
146	Record of conversation: Jobert, Heath and Douglas-Home at 10 Downing Street MWE 3/304/1	2 July	Jobert's talks with Kissinger.
147	Minute: Overton to Hankey AMU 3/507/1	2 July	Covers note on US preoccupations: Kissinger's proposals 'at least 5 0% domestically orientated'.
148	Minute: Parsons to Coles NFW 2/4	3 July	Examines prospects for UNSC debate on Arab-Israeli dispute.
149	Tel 1392 to Washington AMU 18/1	5 July	Message from Heath to Nixon on progress towards reconciling US and European interests.
150	Washington tel 2100 Douglas-Home papers	5 July	Message for Trend: Kissinger concerned at delay in European response to 'Year of Europe' proposals.
151	Minute: Overton to Cable AMU 3/507/1	5 July	Considers value of a US/European Declaration.
152	Tel 1406 to Washington AMU 18/1	6 July	Message from Heath to Nixon on East/West relations.
153	Letter: Greenhill to Trend CAB 164/1233	6 July	Letter to Trend covering analysis of US draft declarations on US/European relations.
154	Tel 1422 to Washington AMU 18/1	9 July	Message from Nixon to Heath on progress towards US/European Declaration.
155	Minutes of Cabinet Ministerial Committee on Economic Strategy: ES(73) 5th mtg CAB 134/3606	9 July	Records discussion of cooperation amongst oil consuming states and future energy policy.
156	Letter: Cromer to Greenhill AMU 3/507/1	10 July	Summarises developments bearing on US/European relations.
157	Note by Brimelow MWE 3/304/5	14 July	Recording conversation with Sonnenfeldt regarding Scheel's visit to Washington.

158	Tel 958 to UKREP Brussels MWE 3/304/1	14 July	Reports agreement on questions for ministerial decision.
159	Tel 959 to UKREP Brussels MWE 3/304/1	14 July	Lists questions for Ministers.
160	Tel No. 960 to UKREP Brussels MWE 3/304/1	14 July	Comments on No. 159.
161	White House tel to Cabinet Office AMU 18/1	18 July	Personal message from Nixon to Heath stressing need to put Atlantic relations on a 'firmer basis'.
162	Minute: Cable to Brimelow RS 2/3	18 July	Covers Planning Staff paper on transatlantic relations.
163	Tel 561 to Paris MWE 3/304/1	18 July	Seeks Jobert's views on likely response to questions in No. 159.
164	Tel 562 to Paris MWE 3/304/1	18 July	Text of paper on US/European relations.
165	Record of conversation: Douglas-Home/Brunner MWE 3/304/1	18 July	Discussion of Scheel's Washington visit.
166	Paris tel 962 MWE 3/304/1	20 July	Assesses French position on European response to Kissinger's initiative.
167	Tel 1528 to Washington MWE 3/304/1	24 July	Reports progress made at ministerial meeting of the Nine.
168	Tel 1529 to Washington MWE 3/304/1	24 July	Transmits press communiqué of ministerial meeting.
169	Tel 1530 to Washington MWE 3/304/1	24 July	Reports points agreed by the Correspondants of the Nine.
170	Tel 1531 to Washington MWE 3/304/1	24 July	Summarises main points made in ministerial discussion.
171	Letter: Palliser to J O Wright MWE 3/304/1	24 July	Reports Jobert's claims that HMG was not keeping partners informed on UK/US relations.
172	Minute: Amery to Douglas-Home NFW 2/4	25 July	Criticises British position in UNSC Arab-Israeli debate.
173	Minute: Douglas-Home to	26 July	Response to No. 172.

Amery
NFW 2/4

174	Tel 1548 to Washington AMU 18/1	26 July	Message from Heath to Nixon reporting results of Copenhagen ministerial meeting.
175	UKMIS New York tel 764 NFW 2/4	26 July	Reports on UNSC debate on Arab-Israeli dispute and application of US veto.
176	DTI memo for Cabinet Official Committee on Europe: EUO(73) 145 SMG 12/598/1	26 July	Outlines UK objectives and EC energy policy.
177	Minute: Parsons to Acland NFW 2/4	27 July	Analyses UNSC debate on Arab-Israeli dispute.
178	Tel 1567 to Washington RS 2/3	27 July	Message from Nixon to Heath expressing irritation at outcome of Copenhagen ministerial meeting.
179	Record of meeting: Kissinger/Trend RS 2/3	30 July	Discussion of US/European relations: Kissinger warns Trend against the development of 'adversary relationship'.

3 August – 3 October 1973

180	Ottawa tel 27 to Washington MWE 3/304/1	3 Aug	Message from Heath to Nixon expressing determination to reaffirm 'purposes and vitality of the Atlantic relationship'.
181	Ottawa tel 3 to Paris MWE 3/304/1	3 Aug	Informs of forthcoming message to Brandt and Pompidou.
182	Ottawa tel 4 to Paris MWE 3/304/1	3 Aug	Text of message from Heath suggesting a meeting with Brandt and Pompidou to consider whether to promote a European initiative towards USA.
183	Tel 288 to UKDEL NATO MWE 3/304/6	3 Aug	Instructs on handling of draft text of proposed NATO Declaration.
184	Tel 289 to UKDEL NATO MWE 3/304/6	3 Aug	Draft NATO Declaration.
185	Bonn tel 7 to Ottawa MWE 3/304/1	3 Aug	Germans thought that a top-level meeting before Copenhagen would be 'too dramatic'.

186	Tel 512 to Ottawa MWE 3/304/1	6 Aug	Reports Brimelow's briefing of EC Ambassadors on Trend's talks with Kissinger.
187	Letter: Reeve to R M Hunt NB 12/1	7 Aug	Reports meeting with ARAMCO representative: Saudi reactions to UNSC debate.
188	Tel 531 to Ottawa MWE 3/304/1	8 Aug	Text of Brandt's reply to Heath's message in No 182.
189	Paris tel 4 to Ottawa MWE 3/304/1	8 Aug	Translation of Pompidou's reply to Heath's message.
190	Paris tel 1044 MWE 3/304/1	8 Aug	Informs that the French were not sorry to see the US initiative 'bogged down'.
191	Tel 188 to Copenhagen MWE 3/304/1	8 Aug	Informs of forthcoming draft US/EC communiqué and ideas on European identity paper.
192	Tel 189 to Copenhagen MWE 3/304/1	8 Aug	Text of draft EC/US communiqué.
193	FCO paper MWE 3/304/1	undated	Identity of the Nine *vis-à-vis* US.
194	Ottawa tel 4 to Bonn MWE 3/304/1	8 Aug	Message from Heath to Brandt: Brimelow to visit Bonn.
195	Ottawa tel 7 to Paris MWE 3/304/1	8 Aug	Message from Heath to Pompidou: proposes Brimelow should visit Paris.
196	Washington tel 29 to Ottawa MWE 3/304/1	8 Aug	Informs Greenhill of Kissinger's comments on Brimelow's briefing of EC Ambassadors.
197	Bonn tel 867 MWE 3/304/1	9 Aug	Reports Brandt's views on tripartite official discussions with the French.
198	Letter: Brimelow to Stark CAB 164/1235	10 Aug	Informs of handling US draft Declaration.
199	Letter: Sykes to Brimelow File destroyed	13 Aug	Analyses Kissinger's criticisms of British diplomacy.
200	Bonn tel 895 MWE 3/304/1	17 Aug	Reports Brimelow/Scheel talks on responding to Kissinger.
201	Paris tel 1092 MWE 3/304/1	20 Aug	Analyses French attitude towards an EC/US declaration.

202	Paris tel 1093 MWE 3/304/1	20 Aug	Suggests basis of a declaration acceptable to the French.
203	Letter: Sykes to Brimelow AMU 3/507/1	22 Aug	Assesses US position regarding transatlantic relations.
204	Letter: H B Walker to P R H Wright NBS 12/1	23 Aug	Considers seriousness of Arab threat to use the 'oil weapon'.
205	Paris tel 1112 MWE 3/304/1	24 Aug	Reports French preparations for forthcoming meeting of Nine Foreign Ministers at Copenhagen.
206	Tel 637 to Paris MWE 3/304/1	24 Aug	Responds favourably to ideas outlined in Nos. 201 and 202.
207	Washington tel 2647 MWE 3/304/1	24 Aug	Reports Kissinger's statement on projected Nixon visit to Europe.
208	Minute: Overton to Wiggin AMU 3/507/1	24 Aug	Records conversation with A James of US Embassy on tabling in NATO of draft Declaration.
209	Tel 640 to Paris MWE 3/304/1	27 Aug	Reports Heath's conversation with Jobert, and latter's support for British draft Declaration.
210	Paris tel 1122 MWE 3/304/1	28 Aug	Reports conversation with Puaux on draft Declaration: French preparing to accept a 'fairly anodyne text'.
211	Minute: Alexander to Cable MWE 3/304/1	28 Aug	Transcript of Douglas-Home's manuscript minute on No. 179.
212	Paris tel 1126 MWE 3/304/1	29 Aug	Reports Brimelow's discussion of British draft Declaration with Jobert and French officials.
213	Tel 1770 to Washington MWE 3/304/1	31 Aug	Reports Correspondants' Group consensus on use of the British draft Declaration.
214	Letter: Sykes to Overton AMU 1/2	31 Aug	Assesses significance of Kissinger's nomination as Secretary of State.
215	Tel 649 to Paris AMU 3/507/1	1 Sep	Stresses importance of achieving consensus amongst the Nine.
216	Paris tel 1146 AMU 3/507/1	3 Sep	Reports that French would take British draft as basis for Declaration.
217	Letter: Bridges to	4 Sep	Covers text of message from

	Alexander AMU 18/1		Heath to Nixon: next Copenhagen meeting might prove a 'new point of departure'.
218	Paris tel 1149 AMU 3/507/1	4 Sep	Reports Jobert/Armstrong conversation: Jobert 80% confident of agreement at Copenhagen.
219	Copenhagen tel 320 MWE 3/304/1	5 Sep	J O Wright reports that Political Directors' meeting went well.
220	Copenhagen tel 322 MWE 3/304/1	5 Sep	Transmits outline text of EC/US Declaration of Principles.
221	Tel 1815 to Washington AMU 3/507/1	6 Sep	Instructs Cromer to tell Kissinger of progress on draft Declaration.
222	Tel 1816 to Washington AMU 3/507/1	6 Sep	Conveys proposed procedures for Nixon's visit to Europe.
223	Washington tel 2767 AMU 3/507/1	7 Sep	Sykes reports talk with Sonnenfeldt regarding No. 222.
224	Cairo despatch 1/1 NFW 3/322/1	7 Sep	Adams concludes that Sadat is 'man of peace'.
225	Nixon tel to Heath AMU 18/1	9 Sep	Responds to message in No. 217.
226	Copenhagen tel 335 AMU 3/507/1	11 Sep	Douglas-Home informs Heath that ministerial meeting of Nine went well.
227	Copenhagen tel 339 AMU 3/507/1	11 Sep	Douglas-Home reports progress with transatlantic dialogue.
228	Tel 240 to Copenhagen AMU 3/507/1	17 Sep	Reports Kissinger's reactions to results of Copenhagen meeting.
229	Washington tel 2920 AMU 3/507/1	19 Sep	Reports US criticisms of conduct of the Nine.
230	Tel 1918 to Washington AMU 22/3	20 Sep	Douglas-Home's plans for meeting with Kissinger.
231	Minute: Cable to Acland RS 2/3	21 Sep	Covers Planning Staff paper analysing impact of the 'Year of Europe' initiative.
232	Draft record of conversation: Douglas-Home and Kissinger New York AMU 3/548/15	24 Sep	The 'Year of Europe': Kissinger complains about European response to the US initiative.
233	Tel Aviv tel 402 NFW 3/408/1	25 Sep	Reports conversation with Eban on prospects for Arab-Israeli

negotiations.

234	UKMIS New York tel 961 AMU 3/507/1	25 Sep	Andersen's account of meeting with Kissinger.
235	UKMIS New York tel 1018 MWE 3/304/6	29 Sep	J O Wright reports talks between Political Committee of the Nine and American officials.
236	UKMIS New York tel 1019 MWE 3/304/6	29 Sep	Text of draft EC/US Declaration with American amendments.
237	UKMIS New York tel 1020 MWE 3/304/6	29 Sep	American comments on amended draft Declaration.
238	Washington tel 3040 MWE 3/304/1	1 Oct	Conversation with Stoessel: US wished to continue EC/US dialogue in a 'conciliatory spirit'.
239	Letter: Cromer to Brimelow MWE 3/304/1	2 Oct	Americans seemed ready to build upon what the Europeans had achieved at Copenhagen.
240	Tel 1195 to UKREP Brussels AMU 3/507/1	3 Oct	Expresses desire for common European position by 18 October.
241	Tel 1196 to UKREP Brussels AMU 3/507/1	3 Oct	Comments on US proposed amendments to draft Declaration.

5 October – 14 November 1973

242	Tel Aviv tel FOH 05100Z to MoD NFW 10/9	5 Oct	Defence Attaché reports Israeli assessment of Egyptian and Syrian military preparations.
243	Washington tel 3093 MWE 3/304/1	5 Oct	Reports on Kissinger's talk with Thorn about EC/US relations.
244	Tel Aviv tel FOH 060945Z to MoD NFW 10/9	6 Oct	Reports Israeli partial mobilisation following evacuation of Soviet personnel.
245	Cairo tel 742 NFW 10/9	6 Oct	Reports rumours of troop recalls.
246	Tel Aviv tel FOH 061100Z to MoD NFW 10/9	6 Oct	Defence Attaché reports military briefing that moment might be 'propitious' for Arab attack.
247	Tel Aviv tel FOH 061242Z to MoD NFW 10/9	6 Oct	Egyptian and Syrian forces were attacking in Sinai and on the Golan Heights.

248	Tel 313 to Tel Aviv NFW 10/9	6 Oct	Informs of call for UNSC meeting; UK arms supplies to combatants suspended.
249	Washington tel 3117 NFW 10/9	6 Oct	Reports Kissinger's request for cooperation.
250	Washington tel 3118 NFW 10/9	6 Oct	Reports that Cromer had told Kissinger that UK could not support call for Arab withdrawal.
251	Cairo tel 751 NFW 10/9	7 Oct	Reports Sadat's warning that Egypt would not accept ceasefire 'until all Arab territory had been regained'.
252	Tel 505 to Cairo NFW 10/9	7 Oct	Parsons informed Arab League Ambassadors of HMG's objective to bring fighting to an end.
253	Washington tel 3122 NFW 10/9	7 Oct	Reports Kissinger intention to press on with UNSC resolution.
254	Minute: M D Butler to Acland MWE 3/304/6	8 Oct	Records Anglo-French discussion of transatlantic relations.
255	Minute: Alexander to M D Butler MWE 3/304/6	9 Oct	Transcript of note by Douglas-Home expressing hope that Nixon would visit in November.
256	Minute: J J B Hunt to Heath NB 12/5	9 Oct	Notes views of Task Force on Oil Supplies on current situation.
257	UKDEL NATO tel 653 WDN 26/304/3	10 Oct	Transatlantic relations: US acceptance of French draft as basis for Declaration.
258	Tel 520 to Cairo NFW 10/9	11 Oct	Questioned whether time right for proposing cease-fire.
259	Minute: Parsons to Alexander NFW 2/28	11 Oct	Analyses British objectives in the Middle East crisis.
260	Damascus tel 68 NFW 10/9	11 Oct	Informs of military situation on the Syrian front.
261	Cairo tel 796 NFW 10/9	11 Oct	Reports indications of opinion in favour of cease-fire.
262	Amman tel 511 NFW 10/9	11 Oct	Reports pressure on Jordan for military assistance to Syria.
263	Cairo tel 797 NFW 10/9	11 Oct	Reports encouraging Hatim to think in terms of cease-fire.

264	Tel Aviv tel FOH 112020Z to MoD NFW 10/9	11 Oct	Reports Israeli assessment of military situation.
265	Tel 299 to Amman NFW 10/9	11 Oct	Message from Douglas-Home to King Hussein: sympathises with Jordan's predicament.
266	Tel 184 to The Hague SMG 6/1	11 Oct	Informs that OPEC/oil company negotiations are in a 'critical phase'.
267	Washington tel 3183 NFW 2/29	12 Oct	Kissinger asks UK to propose a UNSC cease-fire *in situ* resolution.
268	Tel 345 to Jedda File destroyed	12 Oct	Heath issues warning of need to avoid imperilling oil supplies.
269	Washington tel 3187 NFW 2/29	12 Oct	Reports Kissinger's telephone message regarding cease-fire resolution: Israelis 'might play'.
270	Tel 2076 to Washington NFW 2/29	12 Oct	Expresses doubts as to whether Egypt or Israel would be interested in *in situ* cease-fire.
271	Washington tel 3199 MWE 3/304/1	12 Oct	Account of Jobert's meeting with Kissinger: transatlantic relations.
272	Washington tel 3200 NFW 10/9	12 Oct	Reports that Kissinger was 'gratified' by HMG's 'positive response' to his UNSC proposal.
273	Cairo tel 820 NFW 10/9	13 Oct	Reports conditions on which Egypt would accept a cease-fire.
274	Cairo tel 821 NFW 10/9	13 Oct	Sadat denounces 'Kissinger trick'.
275	Tel 536 to Cairo NFW 10/9	13 Oct	Instructs Ambassador to enquire again as to Sadat's attitude towards a cease-fire resolution.
276	Minute: Gore-Booth to Parsons NFW 2/29	13 Oct	Reports telephone conversation in which Kissinger pressed Douglas-Home to proceed with resolution.
277	Washington tel 3201 NFW 10/9	13 Oct	Kissinger complains of 'unsatisfactory' telephone conversation with Douglas-Home.
278	Washington tel 3202 NFW 10/9	13 Oct	Cromer advises FCO to consult the Russians on Egypt's position.
279	Cairo tel 832	13 Oct	Reports that Sadat was opposed

NFW 10/9 | to proposed UNSC resolution, and that he would ask the Chinese to veto it.

280 Record of meeting at Chequers: Heath, Douglas-Home and officials
NFW 10/9 | 13 Oct | Discussion of Kissinger's proposal for UK-sponsored cease-fire resolution.

281 Record of telephone conversation: Douglas-Home/Kissinger
NFW 10/9 | 13 Oct | Douglas-Home relates that he and Heath did not think the time ripe for Kissinger's proposed UNSC initiative.

282 Washington tel 3208A
NFW 10/9 | 13 Oct | Reports Kissinger's criticism of British stance on a cease-fire resolution and US readiness to start 'massive resupply' of Israel.

283 Washington tel 3209
NFW 10/9 | 13 Oct | Expresses view that Kissinger's 'strong language' reflected Nixon's feelings.

284 Washington tel 3210
NFW 10/9 | 13 Oct | Reports further telephone call from Kissinger to explain Soviet position.

285 Washington tel 3211
Douglas-Home papers | 14 Oct | Reflects on the 'absence of forward thinking' by Kissinger and Nixon.

286 Tel 540 to Cairo
NFW 10/9 | 14 Oct | Reports that Greenhill had told the Soviet Ambassador that a cease-fire must be the first step towards a final settlement.

287 Minute: Gore-Booth to Parsons
NFW 10/9 | 15 Oct | Covers letter from Weir regarding US facilities for re-supply of Israel.

288 Tel 2081 to Washington
SMG 6/1 | 15 Oct | Message from Heath to Nixon expressing concern about oil supply and prices.

289 Cairo tel 855
NFW 10/9 | 15 Oct | Adams thought buffer zone idea represented best chance of peace.

290 Tel 2084 to Washington
AMU 3/507/1 | 15 Oct | Suggests NATO summit to mark the alliance's 25th anniversary.

291 Guidance tel 159
AMU 3/507/1 | 15 Oct | Summarises progress with the 'Year of Europe'.

292 Guidance tel 160
AMU 3/507/1 | 15 Oct | Examines impact of emerging common foreign policy of the Nine on transatlantic relations.

293	Tel 542 to Cairo NFW 10/9	15 Oct	Reports Egyptian Ambassador's thanks for HMG's attitude towards the Arab-Israeli conflict.
294	Tel Aviv tel 479 NFW 10/9	16 Oct	Reports conversation with Peres: 'things are grim'.
295	Tel 339 to Tel Aviv NFW 10/9	16 Oct	Douglas-Home outlines proposals for international guarantees of Israel's security.
296	Jedda tel 492 MWE 2/12	16 Oct	Reports Saudi threat to cut back oil production.
297	Minute: J A Thomson to Parsons File destroyed	16 Oct	Confirms US assurances that Israel would not be re-supplied from the UK.
298	Cabinet minutes: CM(73) 46th conclusions, minute 2 CAB 128/53	16 Oct	Douglas-Home sums up the situation in the Middle East.
299	UKDEL NATO tel 668 WDN 26/24	16 Oct	Reports on NAC meeting on the implications of the Arab-Israeli war.
300	UKDEL NATO tel 669 WDN 26/24	16 Oct	Rumsfeld's statements in the NAC.
301	Tel 351 to Jedda NB 12/5	16 Oct	Responds to Saudi oil warning in No. 296, and points out risk of alienating Western Europe.
302	Minute: Douglas-Home to Heath MWE 3/304/1	17 Oct	Recommends to his colleagues the study of the 'Year of Europe' at No. 231.
303	Tel 2095 to Washington Douglas-Home papers	17 Oct	Seeks information on US/Soviet relations and the Middle Eastern war.
304	Minutes of Cabinet Working Party on Oil Supplies, WP(OS) (73) 2nd mtg SMG 12/548/9	18 Oct	Records discussion of latest developments regarding Arab oil production.
305	Cabinet minutes: CM(73) 48th conclusions, minute 2 CAB 128/53	18 Oct	Discussion of current developments in the Middle Eastern conflict.
306	Washington tel 3257 Douglas-Home papers	18 Oct	Reports on Kissinger's contacts with the Russians on the Middle East.
307	Copenhagen tel 417	19 Oct	Reports on meeting of the Nine's

	MWE 3/304/6		Political Committee with EC Commission and US representatives to discuss US/Nine Declaration.
308	Copenhagen tel 418 MWE 3/304/6	19 Oct	Assesses significance of Copenhagen meeting.
309	UKDEL NATO tel 683 WDN 26/24	19 Oct	Reports NAC meeting: Rumsfeld expresses US view on the role of allies in the Middle East.
310	Cairo tel FOH 191530Z to MoD NWF 10/9	19 Oct	Reports establishment of Israeli bridgehead on the west bank of the Suez Canal.
311	Washington tel 3284 Douglas-Home papers	19 Oct	Informs of Kissinger's impending visit to Moscow.
312	Tel 788 to Moscow File destroyed	20 Oct	Instructs Killick to inform Kissinger of HMG's hopes for an immediate cease-fire.
313	Tel 2118 to Washington AMU 18/1	20 Oct	Message from Nixon to Heath proposing discussions on oil supplies and prices.
314	Tel Aviv tel 500 NFW 10/9	20 Oct	Expresses doubts about Israeli readiness to accept balanced cease-fire.
315	Washington tel 3289 SMG 12/5	20 Oct	Concludes that Americans were 'clearly rattled' by developments.
316	Tel 790 to Moscow File destroyed	21 Oct	Expresses Douglas-Home's wish for meeting with Kissinger.
317	Tel 2119 to Washington AMU 18/1	21 Oct	Message from Heath to Nixon responding positively to No. 313.
318	Moscow tel 1220 PREM 15/1766	21 Oct	Reports US/Soviet agreement on joint tabling of UNSC resolution.
319	Moscow tel 1221 File destroyed	21 Oct	Reports Kissinger's account of US/Soviet talks.
320	Minute: Carrington to Heath Douglas-Home papers	22 Oct	Informs of discussion by Task Force on Oil Supplies on possible cooperation within OECD.
321	Tel 2127 to Washington File destroyed	23 Oct	Account of London talks with Kissinger on prospects for Middle Eastern peace.
322	Washington tel 3299 NFW 10/16	23 Oct	Warns Douglas-Home that US did not appreciate importance of Arab oil to Europeans.

323	Minute: R T Armstrong to Caines NB 12/5	23 Oct	Informs DTI that BP would not be surprised if instructed not to fulfil contracts to US.
324	Tel 2138 to Washington NFW 10/16	24 Oct	Stresses importance of oil to the European economy.
325	Tel Aviv tel 519 NFW 10/9	24 Oct	Records discussion with Eban of British stance during the war.
326	Tel Aviv tel 520 NFW 10/9	24 Oct	Foresees a 'new flexibility' in Israeli attitude towards a Middle Eastern settlement.
327	Tel 2140 to Washington NFW 10/16	24 Oct	Suggests steps towards achieving peace in the Middle East.
328	Washington tel 3327 NFW 10/16	25 Oct	Reports conversation with Kissinger on cease-fire implementation and follow-up.
329	Washington tel 3328 Douglas-Home papers	25 Oct	Informs of US decision to go on to a 'low level military alert' in response to threat of Soviet military intervention.
330	Tel 2143 to Washington Douglas-Home papers	25 Oct	Instructs Cromer to tell Kissinger that Brezhnev might have to act to save the Egyptians and his own prestige.
331	Cabinet minutes (extract): CM(73) 49th conclusions, minute 1 NFW 10/9	25 Oct	Douglas-Home explains current developments regarding the cease-fire.
332	UKDEL NATO tel 696 Douglas-Home papers	25 Oct	Reports Rumsfeld's statement in the NAC regarding the US 'alert'.
333	Washington tel 3331 Douglas-Home papers	25 Oct	Reports Kissinger's views on a further UNSC resolution.
334	Letter: Cromer to Douglas-Home Douglas-Home papers	25 Oct	Considers the impact of Watergate on Kissinger's diplomacy.
335	Tel 809 to Moscow Douglas-Home papers	25 Oct	Message from Heath to Brezhnev deprecating unilateral military intervention in the Middle East.
336	Washington tel 3343 NFW 2/29	25 Oct	Reports Kissinger's expressed hope that peace negotiations might begin in 2-3 weeks.
337	Moscow tel 1251	26 Oct	Reports conversation with

	MWE 2/12		Gromyko: Sadat's response to Heath's proposals in No. 335.
338	Moscow tel 1252 MWE 2/12	26 Oct	Gromyko requests clarification of Heath's proposals on cease-fire implementation.
339	Tel 2152 to Washington NFW 2/29	26 Oct	Stresses importance of defusing 'critical danger spot'.
340	Cairo tel FOH 261630Z to MoD File destroyed	26 Oct	Defence Attaché reports Sadat's demands for Israeli withdrawal to 22 October positions.
341	Cairo tel 993 NFW 2/29	26 Oct	Reports Ismail Fahmy's fears of a superpower deal.
342	Washington tel 3367 NFW 2/29	26 Oct	Reports indications that Americans now favoured earlier start to peace negotiations.
343	Tel Aviv tel 535 NFW 2/29	27 Oct	Assesses Israeli attitude towards negotiations.
344	Tel 594 to Cairo NFW 2/29	27 Oct	Outlines British position on peace negotiations.
345	Washington tel 3377 File destroyed	27 Oct	Informs of Sisco's assessment of cease-fire implementation.
346	Washington tel 3378 NFW 2/29	27 Oct	Stresses need to maintain momentum in peace process.
347	The Hague tel 493 NB 12/2	29 Oct	Reports Dutch concern over impact of Arab oil embargo.
348	The Hague tel 494 NB 12/2	29 Oct	Suggests sympathetic approach to Dutch oil needs.
349	Letter: Douglas-Home to Cromer Douglas-Home papers	30 Oct	Expresses concern over impact of Watergate on Nixon's authority.
350	Tel 2186 to Washington NFW 2/29	31 Oct	Text of draft message from Heath to Nixon on the need for early start to peace negotiations.
351	Washington tel 3415 NFW 2/29	31 Oct	Reports Kissinger's assurances on future peace negotiations.
352	Washington tel 3416 NFW 2/29	31 Oct	Reports Kissinger's complaints over lack of European support.
353	Guidance tel 170 SMG 12/548/4	31 Oct	Assesses possible impact of the Arab oil embargo.
354	Tel 2197 to Washington	31 Oct	Reports discussion between

	MWE 3/304/1		Stoessel and J O Wright of US/European differences.
355	Bonn tel 1165 MWE 3/304/6	1 Nov	Reports Kissinger was 'bored' with EC/US Declaration.
356	Minute: Fenn to Parsons MWE 2/12	1 Nov	Analyses UK oil supplies and the European problem.
357	Tel 196 to The Hague NB 12/2	1 Nov	Explains that immediate concern must be to avoid putting Europe's remaining oil supplies at risk.
358	Tel 197 to The Hague NB 12/2	1 Nov	Message from Douglas-Home to van der Stoel: advises against giving appearance of EC concerted action on oil.
359	The Hague tel 505 NB 12/2	2 Nov	Reports van der Stoel's reaction to message at No. 357.
360	Minute: Cable to J O Wright MWE 2/12	2 Nov	Cautions against differences with EC partners over oil.
361	Letter: Cromer to J O Wright AMU 3/507/1	2 Nov	Warns Wright of extent of US displeasure with Europe.
362	Tel 2207 to Washington NFW 2/30	2 Nov	Insists on Europe having a role in the Middle East.
363	Washington tel 3479 NFW 10/11	2 Nov	Reports Kissinger's briefing on the Middle East.
364	Tel 838 to Moscow Douglas-Home papers	3 Nov	Reports Heath/Lunkov meeting: peacemaking in the Middle East.
365	Brief by Middle East Unit MWE 2/12	3 Nov	Outlines issues for forthcoming meeting of the Nine's Political Committee on the Middle East.
366	Washington tel 3483 Douglas-Home papers	4 Nov	Telephone conversation with Kissinger on the peace process.
367	Tel 2218 to Washington Douglas-Home papers	4 Nov	Complains of 'sustained criticism' from US 'official sources'.
368	Record of conversation: Heath/Lunkov NFW 2/29	5 Nov	Lunkov offers Soviet account of Kissinger's Moscow talks.
369	Tel 2222 to Washington Douglas-Home papers	5 Nov	Stresses importance of agreement on cease-fire lines.
370	Washington tel 3494	5 Nov	Considers problems facing

	Douglas-Home papers		Kissinger in the peace process.
371	UKDEL NATO tel 736 NFW 10/11	5 Nov	Objects to Kissinger's claims regarding consultation with allies.
372	UKREP Brussels tel 5321 NFW 2/30	5 Nov	Reports Douglas-Home/van der Stoel discussion of EC response to the Arab oil embargo.
373	Washington tel 3496 Douglas-Home papers	5 Nov	Reports conversation with Rush about US criticisms of allies.
374	Letter: Cromer to Brimelow AMU 3/548/13	6 Nov	Suggests a European initiative 'aimed at lifting US/European relations out of their present dangerous state'.
375	Brussels tel 508 SMG 1/4	6 Nov	Text of Declaration of EC states on the Middle East.
376	Tel 2232 to Washington SMG 12/5	6 Nov	Reports on discussions with Casey on oil supplies.
377	UKREP Brussels tel 5338 SMG 1/4	6 Nov	Informs of European Council discussion on oil supplies.
378	Record of meeting: officials and oil company representatives NB 12/2	7 Nov	Discussion about oil supplies: British desire to work for a joint EC position.
379	Minute: Acland to Parsons NFW 2/29	8 Nov	With minutes by Parsons and Wiggin, covers record of discussion between Carrington and Schlesinger of transatlantic differences.
380	Cairo tel 1121 NFW 2/29	8 Nov	Reports on Kissinger's Middle Eastern diplomacy and hopes for a peace conference.
381	Kuwait tel 1086 NB 12/5	8 Nov	Points to possible threats to British oil supplies.
382	Cairo tel 1122 NFW 2/29	8 Nov	Reports Kissinger's criticism of joint statement of the Nine.
383	Cabinet minutes (extract): CM(73) 53rd conclusions, minute 2 CAB 128/53	8 Nov	Discussion of progress towards implementing the cease-fire and opening peace negotiations.
384	Letter: Adams to Parsons NFW 2/29	9 Nov	Reports Kissinger's retrospective remarks about HMG's response to US cease-fire proposals.
385	Tel 207 to The Hague	10 Nov	Proposes using the Nine's

	MWE 2/12		Declaration in a concerted effort to assist the Netherlands.
386	Paris tel 1543 MWE 2/12	11 Nov	Reports cautious French response to proposed collective démarche.
387	Record of conversation: Heath/Meir NFW 2/29	12 Nov	Prospects for peace in the Middle East.
388	Paris tel 1548 MWE 2/12	12 Nov	Informs that Jobert would prefer 'concerted démarches' to the Arabs on oil supplies.
389	Washington tel 3570 MWE 2/12	12 Nov	Forecasts that proposed European initiative on oil would be seen as 'kow-towing to Arab blackmail'.
390	Letter: Cromer to Adams NFW 2/29	14 Nov	Comments on No. 384.
391	Letter: Cromer to Wiggin NFW 2/29	14 Nov	Analyses US policy towards the Arab-Israeli war.

15 November 1973 – 2 January 1974

392	Letter: Alexander to Bridges MWE 3/304/8	15 Nov	Covers draft English translation of European identity paper.
393	Copenhagen tel 483 MWE 2/12	15 Nov	Reports on meeting of the Political Directors of the Nine and French veto on proposed approach to Arab oil producers.
394	Letter: Cromer to Douglas-Home NFW 2/29	15 Nov	Records conversation with Schlesinger on the deterioration in transatlantic relations.
395	Tel 2298 to Washington NFW 2/29	15 Nov	Reports on talks with Sisco on the Middle East.
396	Washington tel 119 Saving AMU 3/507/1	16 Nov	Assesses impact of the Middle Eastern war on US attitudes towards NATO.
397	Letter: Cromer to Brimelow AMU 3/5071	21 Nov	Outlines response to US criticisms of allies over the Middle Eastern war.
398	Letter: Cromer to Douglas-Home SMG 25/304/1	21 Nov	Informs of discussion with Shultz of the economic consequences of the energy crisis.
399	Letter: Douglas-Home to Cromer	21 Nov	Claims that the 'basic trouble' was the failure of the Americans

	Douglas-Home papers		to decide on 'how far to turn the screw on Israel'.
400	Paris tel 1604 MWE 2/12	22 Nov	Reports Jobert's assent to the démarche to Arab states.
401	Tel 665 to Cairo MWE 2/12	22 Nov	Explains developments amongst the Nine regarding the démarche.
402	Tel 666 to Cairo MWE 2/12	22 Nov	Instructs on the handling of the European démarche.
403	Tel 667 to Cairo MWE 2/12	22 Nov	Transmits text of agreed démarche.
404	Washington tel 3658 AMU 3/507/1	22 Nov	Reports on Kissinger's press conference on the Middle East.
405	Tel 2344 to Washington MWE 3/304/6	22 Nov	Speculates on prospects of a meeting between EC Foreign Ministers and Kissinger.
406	Note by Douglas-Home for Cabinet Ministerial Committee on European Strategy (EUS(73) 9) MWE 1/548/20	23 Nov	Covers paper on the future of EPC.
407	Minute: J O Wright to M D Butler MWE 3/304/6	23 Nov	Argues for early conclusion of EC/US Declaration.
408	Letter: Carrington to Douglas-Home NB 10/13	23 Nov	Proposes contingency planning for possible US resort to military action in the Middle East.
409	Minute: Bullard to Craig NFW 2/29	23 Nov	Warns of the dangers inherent in superpower guarantees of a Middle Eastern settlement.
410	Tel 2354 to Washington AMU 3/507/1	23 Nov	Advises against public recriminations amongst allies.
411	Washington tel 3673 NFW 2/29	24 Nov	Reports Kissinger's views on the prospects for Arab-Israeli peace.
412	Washington tel 3674 AMU 3/507/1	24 Nov	Records Kissinger's complaints over the state of transatlantic relations.
413	Guidance tel 182 MWE 2/12	26 Nov	Assesses current situation in the Middle East.
414	Minute: M D Butler to J O Wright MWE 3/304/6	26 Nov	Rejects Wright's suggestion in No. 407.

	AMU 3/548/14		over press criticism attributed to HMG.
430	Washington tel 3737 AMU 3/548/14	30 Nov	AP report of 'biting [British] attacks' on Kissinger's diplomacy.
431	Tel 2405 to Washington Douglas-Home papers	1 Dec	Offers Kissinger assurance that there was no 'campaign' against him.
432	Washington tel 3752 AMU 3/507/1	2 Dec	Analyses shortcomings of the 'Year of Europe'.
433	Tel 2409 to Washington MWE 3/304/8	3 Dec	J O Wright defends drafting of European identity paper.
434	Report by Joint Intelligence Committee (A) JIC (A) (73) 34 CAB 186/15	5 Dec	Examines the main effects of the Arab-Israeli war and speculates on whether the US might use force to secure oil supplies.
435	UKREP Brussels tel 6054 SMG 12/598/1	5 Dec	Reports EC ministerial discussion of energy problem.
436	Minute: J O Wright to Acland SMG 12/598/1	5 Dec	Informs of preparations for the forthcoming EC summit at Copenhagen.
437	Minute: Goulding to Acland MWE 1/548/25	6 Dec	Records Amery's concern over isolation of Britain and France within the EC on energy matters.
438	Tel 703 to Cairo NB 12/13	6 Dec	Text of message urging Egypt to exercise a moderating influence at meeting of Arab oil ministers.
439	Washington tel 3811 NFW 2/29	6 Dec	Reports on Kissinger's press conference: there was a 'need for new impetus' in NATO.
440	Minute: Egerton to Taylor NB 12/5	6 Dec	Summarises British approaches to Arab oil producers.
441	Minute: Egerton to Craig MWE 1/548/22	7 Dec	Records discussion with French of how Middle East might be tackled at the European summit.
442	Letter: M D Butler to Graham MWE 3/304/8	7 Dec	Covers revised English draft of European identity paper.
443	Minute: Acland to Goulding MWE 1/548/25	10 Dec	Transcribes Douglas-Home's manuscript comments on No. 436.
444	Tel 763 to Bonn MWE 1/548/22	10 Dec	Outlines British thinking on the Middle East for the Copenhagen

summit.

445	Tel 764 to Bonn MWE 1/548/25	10 Dec	Stresses that EC declaration of solidarity on oil could add to energy supply problems.
446	Tel 1505 to UKREP Brussels SMG 6/6	10 Dec	Advises against official criticism of projected 5% cutback in Arab oil supplies.
447	Brussels tel 595 MWE 1/548/23	10 Dec	Douglas-Home reports Kissinger's statement to NATO Ministers on the state of the alliance.
448	UKDEL NATO tel 876 MWE 1/548/25	11 Dec	Reports Douglas-Home/Jobert talks on the summit's handling of energy and the Middle East.
449	UKDEL NATO tel 879 File destroyed	11 Dec	Douglas-Home informs of private meeting of NATO Foreign Ministers.
450	Tel 1523 to UKREP Brussels MWE 3/404/6	11 Dec	Reports that Kissinger favoured a 'shorter and more eloquent' EC/US Declaration.
451	Letter: Drake to P E Walker SMG 1/3	12 Dec	Recommends consumer cooperation on oil prices.
452	UKREP Brussels tel 6266 MWE 1/548/25	12 Dec	Transmits message from Ortoli to Heath outlining EC Commission's proposals on coping with the energy crisis.
453	Minute: P E Walker to Heath Douglas-Home papers	13 Dec	Proposes effort to persuade Arab oil producers to invest in Britain.
454	Minute: P E Walker to Heath Douglas-Home papers	13 Dec	Assesses the oil supply situation after discussions with major companies.
455	Tel 1033 to Washington NFW 2/29	13 Dec	Relates Parsons/Sisco discussion of projected Middle East peace conference.
456	Tel 1533 to UKREP Brussels AMU 12/1	13 Dec	Reports Boardman/Donaldson discussion of Kissinger's energy proposals.
457	Tel 1534 to UKREP Brussels SMG 12/304/3	13 Dec	Summarises Kissinger's proposals for an Energy Action Group (EAG).
458	Tel 1535 to UKREP Brussels	13 Dec	States initial British reactions to Kissinger's proposals in No. 457.

SMG 12/304/3

459	Washington tel 2466 NFW 2/29 O	13 Dec	Reports Kissinger's views on peace talks and oil.
460	Minute: Thomson to Greenhill File destroyed	13 Dec	Argues for positive response to Kissinger initiative.
461	Minute: Douglas-Home to Heath SMG 12/598/1	13 Dec	Advises Heath to work with Brandt in pressing for early EC acceptance of US proposals.
462	DTI brief MWE 1/548/25	13 Dec	Suggests responses to EC Commission and US proposals for consumer cooperation.
463	Tel 2468 to Washington NFW 2/29	13 Dec	Summarises talk with Kissinger on the EC and the Middle East.
464	Cairo tel 1321 NFW 2/29	14 Dec	Conveys Kissinger's assurances to Douglas-Home.
465	Letter: Sohm to Douglas-Home SMG 12/304/3	15 Dec	Covers personal message from Kissinger: Arab reaction to proposed EAG.
466	Tel 1550 to UKREP Brussels SMG 12/598/1	17 Dec	Comments on EC summit statement on energy.
467	Tel 1551 to UKREP Brussels SMG 12/598/1	17 Dec	Outlines British interests in an EC energy policy.
468	Tel 370 to Amman SMG 6/6	17 Dec	States EC position on Middle East peace process.
469	UKDEL OECD tel 109 SMG 12/304/3	17 Dec	Reports US views on proposed EAG.
470	Tel 75 to UKDEL OECD SMG 12/304/3	18 Dec	Explains British stance on Kissinger's proposal.
471	Washington tel 3908 SMG 12/304/3	18 Dec	Warns of dangers of inadequate response to US initiative.
472	UKREP Brussels tel 6420 SMG 12/598/1	19 Dec	Reports Douglas-Home's refusal to proceed with decisions on EC energy policy.
473	UKREP Brussels tel 6421 SMG 12/598/1	19 Dec	Text of Douglas-Home's statement to EC Council.
474	Letter: Arculus to Taylor SMG 12/304/3	19 Dec	Stresses need to consider 'apparent conflict' between US and French proposals on energy.

475	Tel Aviv tel 675 NFW 2/29	19 Dec	Reports on Kissinger's talks with the Israelis.
476	UKDEL OECD tel 118 SMG 12/304/3	19 Dec	Reports British support for US energy proposal in OECD.
477	Guidance tel 203 SMG 12/598/1	19 Dec	Summarises European summit discussions on energy policy.
478	Minutes: M D Butler/Parsons MWE 2/12	20 Dec	Consider future of Euro-Arab dialogue.
479	Paris tel 1754 NFW 2/29	20 Dec	Reports Sisco's optimistic views on the Geneva peace talks.
480	Tel 2503 to Washington SMG 12/304/3	20 Dec	Points out UK's role in supporting US energy proposals.
481	Tel 2504 to Washington SMG 12/304/3	20 Dec	Douglas-Home assures Kissinger of support for maintaining the momentum of his initiative.
482	Tel 181 to Algiers SMG 6/6	21 Dec	Outlines British objectives regarding forthcoming OAPEC meeting.
483	Paris tel 1768 SMG 12/304/3	21 Dec	Reports Foreign Ministry desk-level views on Kissinger initiative.
484	Washington tel 3947 SMG 12/304/3	27 Dec	Reports Sykes/Donaldson discussion of EAG.
485	Cabinet Office tel to the White House Douglas-Home papers	30 Dec	Message from Heath to Nixon giving personal account of Copenhagen summit.
486	Tel 2539 to Washington SMG 12/304/3	31 Dec	Personal message from Kissinger requesting Douglas-Home's views on impact of oil price rises.
487	Tel 2 to Washington ME 12/548/1	**1974** 2 Jan	Text of Douglas-Home's reply to Kissinger's message in No. 486: EAG could have a 'crucial role'.
488	Minute: M D Butler to Wiggin MWP 3/304/1	2 Jan	Covers draft summary paper, analysing recent developments in transatlantic relations.

3 January – 15 March 1974

489	Minute: Grattan to Bridges ME 12/304/1	3 Jan	Points out that there was no concerted EC view on representation in EAG.

490	Minute: J J B Hunt to Heath Douglas-Home papers	3 Jan	Examines problems that US military intervention in the Middle East could pose.
491	Washington tel 41 ME 12/304/1	4 Jan	Reports discussion of EAG with Flanigan and Eberle.
492	Cairo diplomatic report 86/74 NFX 10/2	7 Jan	Analyses 4th Arab-Israeli war: Egypt had achieved most of its immediate objectives.
493	Washington tel 82 ME 12/304/1	8 Jan	Reports discussion with Simon of a proposed ministerial meeting on energy.
494	Letter: Sohm to Heath ME 12/304/1	9 Jan	Covers invitation to energy conference and letter to OPEC leaders regarding this.
495	Letter: Sohm to Brimelow ME 12/304/1	9 Jan	Covers brief explanation of message at No. 494.
496	Washington despt 4/2 AMU 3/548/9	9 Jan	Assesses the impact of the Middle Eastern war on UK/US relations.
497	Tel 57 to Washington NFX 2/598/1	9 Jan	Instructs Cromer to tell Kissinger of discussion of the Middle East at forthcoming EC Directors' meeting.
498	Letter: Brimelow to Cromer AMU 3/548/3	10 Jan	Covers FCO circular on consultations with the US.
499	Paris tel 39 ME 12/304/1	10 Jan	Reports French desire for concerted EC response to US energy proposals.
500	Washington tel 126 NFX 2/598/1	10 Jan	Advises that a Euro-Arab conference would be viewed in US as counter to Nixon's ideas.
501	Paris tel 40 ME 12/304/1	11 Jan	Summarises French reservations regarding proposed Energy Conference.
502	Tel 19 to Paris ME 12/304/1	11 Jan	Argues in favour of positive response to Nixon's proposals.
503	UKREP Brussels tel 168 ME 12/304/1	11 Jan	Reports COREPER discussion of Energy Conference.
504	Washington tel 137 ME 12/304/1	11 Jan	Reports Kissinger and Simon joint press conference on Nixon proposals.

505	Paris tel 44 ME 12/304/1	12 Jan	Informs of Jobert's dislike of Kissinger proposals.
506	Washington valedictory despatch AMU 12/1	15 Jan	Assesses US domestic situation and overseas relations.
507	Tel 110 to Washington NFX 2/598/1	16 Jan	Reports EC Political Directors' decision to proceed with Euro-Arab dialogue.
508	Cairo diplomatic report 125/74 NFX 10/2	16 Jan	Assesses political results of the 4th Arab-Israeli war.
509	Tel 120 to Washington ME 12/304/1	17 Jan	Informs of decision of EC Council of Ministers to accept Nixon's conference invitation.
510	Tel 121 to Washington ME 12/304/1	17 Jan	Transmits message from Heath to Nixon, accepting conference invitation.
511	Washington tel 193 AMU 3/548/1	17 Jan	Reports Cromer's farewell call on Nixon.
512	DTI note for Cabinet GEN 138(74) 1 CAB 130/641	18 Jan	Examines scope for industrial cooperation between the EC and oil producers.
513	Letter: Brimelow to Sykes AMU 3/507/1	18 Jan	Encloses FCO paper assessing Kissinger's recent European visit.
514	Record of conversation: Douglas-Home/Kissinger MWP 3/304/1	20 Jan	Discussion of the Middle Eastern peace process and the proposed Energy Conference.
515	Minutes of Cabinet European Unit EUU(74) 2nd mtg CAB 134/3761	23 Jan	Discussion of current 'malaise within the Community'.
516	Tel 96 to UKREP Brussels ME 12/598/1	24 Jan	Emphasises HMG's support for the proposed Energy Conference as a means of ensuring US cooperation.
517	UKREP Brussels diplomatic report 149/74 MWP 1/1	25 Jan	Considers UK's first year in the EC: the need for a common foreign policy had 'seldom been so blatantly revealed'.
518	Letter: Sykes to Brimelow AMU 3/507/1	25 Jan	Comments on No. 513, and the need for a 'rather more rounded view of American policy'.

519	Tel 219 to Washington ME 12/304/1	29 Jan	Instructs on HMG's views of the role of the Energy Conference.
520	Washington tel 351 ME 12/304/1	29 Jan	Reports on US preparations for Energy Conference.
521	UKDEL NATO tel 45 NFX 2/579/1	30 Jan	Reports NAC discussion of Alliance consultative procedures.
522	Tel 237 to Washington ME 12/304/1	30 Jan	Reports misgivings about US paper on the Energy Conference.
523	Tel 238 to Washington ME 12/304/1	30 Jan	Transmits text of US paper on the Energy Conference.
524	UKREP Brussels tel 571 ME 12/304/1	31 Jan	Reports COREPER discussion of EC Commission draft conference position paper.
525	Tel 251 to Washington ME 12/304/1	31 Jan	Advises on US handling of energy task force proposal.
526	Note by Custis ME 12/598/1	31 Jan	Records discussion between Carrington and Simonet: the EC, energy and the conference.
527	Letter: Egerton to A Campbell ME 12/304/1	1 Feb	Covers US aide-mémoire on the Energy Conference.
528	Bonn tel 184 ME 12/304/1	1 Feb	Reports German pessimism about the Energy Conference.
529	Washington tel 412 ME 12/304/1	1 Feb	Reports discussion with Katz: US had only 'barest outline' of how task force might proceed.
530	White House tel to Cabinet Office ME 12/304/3	3 Feb	Personal message from Nixon to Heath requesting visit from experienced British official.
531	Tel 269 to Washington ME 12/304/1	3 Feb	Criticises US proposal for conference working groups: HMG would prefer 'to seek a limited objective'.
532	Washington tel 434 ME 12/304/1	4 Feb	Reports US response to British procedural proposals.
533	Letter: Bridges to Alexander ME 12/304/3	4 Feb	Covers copy of message from Heath to Nixon: Rampton to visit Washington for talks.
534	UKREP Brussels tel 690 ME 12/304/1	5 Feb	Reports broad agreement in EC Council on revised draft conference mandate.

535	UKREP Brussels tel 691 ME 12/304/1	5 Feb	Transmits text of EC mandate for the Energy Conference.
536	Guidance tel 18 ME 12/9	5 Feb	Summarises British position with regard to bilateral deals with oil producers.
537	Washington tel 478 ME 12/304/1	6 Feb	Reports Kissinger's speech disclaiming any intention of staging confrontation with oil producing nations.
538	Bonn tel 224 MWP 3/304/1	7 Feb	Reports German criticisms in Political Directors' meeting of French 'anti-American' stance.
539	Steering brief ME 12/304/1	7 Feb	UK steering brief for Washington Energy Conference.
540	Washington tel 489 ME 12/304/3	7 Feb	Criticises US draft conference communiqué.
541	Washington tel 490 ME 12/304/3	7 Feb	Transmits text of US draft conference communiqué.
542	Washington tel 491 ME 12/304/3	7 Feb	Reports UK/US discussions on conference procedure.
543	Minute: Overton to Fenn ME 12/304/1	7 Feb	Contends that EC mandate does not require opposition to a task force as such.
544	Paris tel 181 ME 12/304/1	8 Feb	Informs of French desire that Europe should not appear to be 'acting under American auspices'.
545	UKREP Brussels tel 795 ME 12/304/3	8 Feb	Reports discussion with Soames of conference communiqué.
546	Tel 340 to Washington ME 12/304/3	8 Feb	Comments on US draft conference communiqué, and differences over follow-up.
547	Paris tel 185 ME 12/304/1	9 Feb	Analyses French approach to the Energy Conference.
548	Washington tel 540 ME 12/304/1	12 Feb	Reports that the Energy Conference had run into expected difficulty over follow-up.
549	Washington tel 574 ME 12/304/1	13 Feb	Reports failure at Washington to achieve an EC compromise which would include the French.
550	Washington tel 574 ME 12/304/1	13 Feb	Reports French dissent from the conference communiqué.

551	Washington tel 575 ME 12/304/1	13 Feb	Transmits text of agreed conference communiqué.
552	Minute: C M James to Wiggin MWP 3/304/1	14 Feb	Covers minute by Ewart-Biggs on discussion with de Margerie of transatlantic relations.
553	Guidance tel 24 AMU 2/2	14 Feb	Summarises work of the Energy Conference.
554	Record of meeting: J O Wright/Cuvillier Douglas-Home papers	15 Feb	Discussion of the significance of the Energy Conference for the EC's future.
555	Washington tel 612 AMU 2/2	16 Feb	Comments on the broad political implications of the Energy Conference.
556	White House telegram to Cabinet Office ME 12/17	18 Feb	Personal message from Nixon to Heath expressing appreciation of Douglas-Home's role in the Energy Conference.
557	Minute: Braithwaite to M D Butler MWP 3/304/1	20 Feb	Records discussion with US diplomats of the impact of the Energy Conference on the EC and its relations with the US.
558	Tel 436 to Washington AMU 3/548/6	20 Feb	Explains the case for proceeding with Euro-Arab dialogue.
559	Minute: Tomkins to Ewart-Biggs ME 12/17	22 Feb	Records conversation with Balladur on Anglo-French differences over transatlantic relations.
560	Record of meeting: Douglas-Home/Kissinger AMU 3/548/6	26 Feb	Discussion of energy, the Middle East and the Euro-Arab dialogue.
561	Moscow diplomatic report 199/74 NFX 3/303/1	26 Feb	Examines Soviet role during the 4th Arab-Israeli war.
562	Washington diplomatic report 192/74 ME 12/304/1	27 Feb	Summarises and assesses the significance of the Washington Energy Conference.
563	UKDEL NATO tel 108 MWP 3/304/1	4 Mar	Reports Kissinger's warning: 'If Europe were to "float" her foreign policy, the United States would be bound to follow suit.'
564	Minute: Weir to A Campbell NFX 2/598/1	6 Mar	Covers submission from Craig recommending HMG's early agreement to Euro-Arab dialogue.